Peg Leg, Peg Leg
and Other Harelip Stories

Compiled by Juliana Hamilton Chase

Copyright 2023 by Juliana Hamilton Chase. All rights reserved. Printed in the United States of America. No part of this book may be used or reproduced in any manner whatsoever without written permission.
First Edition Printed in Knoxville, Tennessee, USA
Second Edition provided by Crippled Beagle Publishing

Knoxville, Tennessee, USA
www.crippledbeaglepublishing.com

Cover design by Madeline Littleton

Cover photograph: Aunt Anna, Aunt Ruby, and Great-Grandma Janie

Paperback ISBN 978-1-958533-44-4
Hardcover ISBN 978-1-958533-45-1

For information, contact Juliana Chase, 11728 Autumn Leaves Lane, Knoxville, TN 37934.

Let me state right off that the title of this book is in no way meant to offend any amputee or anyone with a disfigurement. I use it only as part of a story about my sister.

Dedicated to
Deana, Ken, Kelley, Jordan, and Leah

Introduction

Storytelling is elevated to an art form on the front porch. Laughter flows as easily as the soft shadows that fall across the yard. Children giggle as they chase fireflies while the grownups sip sweet tea. This is a time of magic. One by one, the children creep up on the porch and find empty places to sit, or they climb onto someone's lap and snuggle, feeling safe in the bosom of a loving family.

As evening hugs the big ole elm tree, the tone of the stories becomes more subdued, and the eyelids of the children grow heavy. Pretty soon, the only noise is the creak of the porch swing and an occasional chuckle from a grownup. The cool night air and the whippoorwills sing the end of a summer day; this is the music that lulls us to complete contentment.

Storytelling has been one of the most important elements in our family. We have fun laughing at others, and we love telling stories on ourselves to allow others to laugh with us. The retelling of a story only makes it better.

The following stories have been collected over the last twenty-five years. I have recorded them as I remembered them. These stories are true, and some may have been s-t-r-e-t-c-h-e-d a little, so take them in the spirit of fun, and enjoy!

Laughter is good medicine.

—*Juliana Hamilton Chase*

Times Have Changed

One day Gene came by while we were all over at Carl's and eating outside. "Things sure have changed," he said." It used to be that people ate in the house and used the toilet in the yard, but now people eat in the yard and use the toilet in the house." —*Nora B.*

Penny and the Old Woman

Penny the hairdresser had this old woman whose hair she did every week, and each time the old woman would come back because she wasn't happy with it. Then Penny would redo the hairstyle. Penny also worked with the local funeral home doing the hair of people who had died. One day they called her and when she went in, she saw that the person's hair she was to do was this same old woman. While she was doing her hair, she said to herself, "Old woman I won't ever have to do your hair again!" Well, the next day it was decided they would do an autopsy on the woman. They had to transport her to Newberry about eighty miles away, and during the autopsy they messed up her hair. They called Penny back to redo it! —*Juli C.*

The Anniversary Gift

This couple had been married for four years, and for four years the husband had forgotten their anniversary. His wife was angry, and she told him, "Tomorrow morning there had better be a package in our driveway with a big bow on it, and it better go from 0-100 in 60 seconds flat." The next morning the wife looked out and sure enough there was a package with a big pink bow on it. She opened the package to see a bathroom scale. –*Juli C.*

50th Wedding Anniversary

Hanna said to her husband Henry, "You know that tomorrow is our 50th wedding anniversary."

Henry said, "Yep."

Hanna said, "I think that we should celebrate by having a nice dinner. Why don't you go out and kill that chicken in the yard, and I'll make chicken and dumplings."

Old Henry replied, "Why would you want to punish that old chicken for what you and I did fifty years ago!"
—*Bobby L.*

Looking For Money

When my brothers Bub and Gene were boys, they heard Daddy tell a story about how Mr. Will Sharpton was remodeling his house and had found money behind the tongue-and-groove boards he tore out of the front room. The next day Mama and Daddy came to visit me and left the boys at home. Bub and Gene decided to look for money in their house. They got an ax and tore out one wall in the living room before Mama and Daddy got home. They didn't find one penny! That was the only time I ever remember Daddy whipping those boys! —*Nora B.*

"Sometimes bad decisions make great stories."
—*Anonymous*

Nora and the Cow

When I was a girl, about fourteen, my dad bought a cow. Now this cow did not like women (she had been handled only by men). Well, this cow had a calf, and Daddy was partitioning off part of the stall where the cow was kept to prevent the calf from nursing. He told me to bring him a hammer. I got the hammer and started in, and that cow gave me a look that said, "Don't come near me."

Annie, John, & Nora Leopard, 1919

I told Daddy that I was afraid to come into the stall, but he yelled at me to bring him the hammer! Well, I started in, and the cow came after me. I raised the hammer and hit that cow right between the eyes! The cow stumbled back and fell! Daddy screamed "GAL, YOU'VE KILLED MY COW!" Well, the cow did not die, and from that day on I was the only one that could handle her, which meant that I had to do all the milking.
—*Nora B.*

The New Cadillac

In Mobile, Alabama, around 1990 (give or take a few years) this man died. In his will he said he wanted his new Cadillac to be sold and the cash to be given to his girlfriend. So, the man's wife put an ad in the newspaper offering the car for $1. When a man read the ad, he thought it was a joke, but his curiosity got the best of him. He called the woman and asked if it was a joke and she said no, it was specified in her husband's will, so she was following his wishes. She sold that new Caddy for one dollar! I first read this in the Birmingham newspaper and Jim Catrett later confirmed it. He knew this lady. —*Juli C.*

The Gift Card

Emmy won an award at kindergarten and received a $25 gift card for Target. The teacher asked her if she understood why she got it and Emmy said, "Because I like to shop at Target." —*Granny Winkey*

Cherry Yum Yum

The day before Thanksgiving, I was going to make my cherry yum yum dessert and discovered I did not have any pecans to put in my crust. I thought, I wish I knew someone I could borrow some pecans from.

    Just then the phone rang, and it was my next-door neighbor Erma, who said, "I have some pecans for you." —*Lottie G.*

Thanksgiving Prayer

October 2008, I had just moved into the old home place, and there was this big old metal gas tank on a stand in the front yard. I kept thinking about getting rid of it. Thanksgiving Day, a truck stopped, and this young man got out an asked if I wanted to get rid of the tank. I said, "Yes" and he asked how much I wanted for it; I told him he could have it if he cleaned out the climbing rose bush, bricks, and rocks around it. He thanked me and said he would come back for it in a few days. He did and did a great job of cleaning up. —*Juli C.*

Smoking in the Cotton Barn

While at the hospital one morning sitting with Bobby, a friend of his started telling stories. This man, Boyce Green, grew up in Windsor, South Carolina, on a farm in 1939. He told how as a boy of four or five his older brother was teaching him how to smoke. They were in the cotton barn and after he lit his cigarette, he flipped the match over in the cotton. Well, the barn caught on fire and burned, and he got the worst whipping of his life. When his Pa went to whip his brother, his brother ran and climbed a pine tree. His Pa told him to come down, but he only climbed higher and refused to come down. Pa told me, "Boy, run get my ax." He did, and his Pa cut down the pine and the brother hit the ground, jumped up, and ran again. He finally did come home that night and took his whipping. —*Juli C.*

The Gas Leak

Uncle Bub had this old Winnebago, and he smelled a gas leak. He did not have a flashlight, so he lit a match and sure enough there was a leak. He blew out the side of his camper! —*Bobby L.*

"If that boy had a brain, he would take it out and play with it!!" —*Old Saying*

Ole Dead Eye

One time Bub had a mouse in his house. He took out Baby (his gun) and shot at the mouse. He missed the mouse, but he got the toilet! —*Nora B.*

Mamma always said that Bub did not get all that was coming to him when he was born.

Sue said, "Bless his heart, he's one brick shy of a full load."

Uncle Bub was the Barney Fife of our family.
—*Marty L.*

What do I do now?

SOB Board

My husband Mickey (a Baptist preacher and building contractor) sent me to the building supply store to pick up some supplies. I walked in and asked for some SOB boards. Well, all those guys started laughing. Living in a small town, they all knew that I was the preacher's wife and would never use foul language. One of the guys called out loud, "The Preacher's wife wants some SOB boards and charge it to the church!" I did not know why they were laughing; Mickey later explained to me that I had transposed the letters. I should have asked for OSB boards. —*Pealey H.*

The Strip Joint

Someone at church asked me where I worked. I said, "Down at the strip joint." The person's eyes got big, and he was speechless. I explained that the Strip Joint was a furniture refinishing shop. Mickey made me quit that job because the owner was a good-looking son-of-a-gun, and Mickey did not trust him. —*Pealey H.*

Brown Hound's Bed

The Old Man had a yard dog, and he was called Brown Hound. Now Brown Hound did not like just anybody. He knew all the family, and did not bother them. One day Doug Feagan come by the house, and he wiped his feet on the rug at the front door. Well, Ole Brown came up off the porch and bit Doug on the ankle! That was where Ole Brown slept, and he would bite anyone who wiped their feet on his bed. —*Bobby L*

Ole Blue

Aunt Tinky had a dog that had a litter of puppies. Mamma told Marty that she could have one of them. Marty said I want that blue one, so that's how Ole Blue got his name. —*Twiddle*

Getting Stuck

Me and John D. went by to visit Bub. Bub had just run his truck down the hill in his back yard, and it was stuck. He said, "I'll go get Jeff [his son who lived next door] to pull me out with his four-wheel drive." Jeff came over and hooked a cable to Bub's bumper. Jeff got in his truck, and Bub got in his and put it in drive. Jeff put his in drive, and they both gunned it! Dirt was flying ten feet high, and neither was going anywhere.

Jeff stopped, got out and yelled, "Daddy if you will put it in reverse, I'll pull you out!" —*Bobby L*

Bear Hunting

This fellow went hunting and came upon a bear. He turned and started running, the whole time praying, "Dear Lord, do not let that bear catch me." He ran until he could not run anymore, and he fell on the ground. The bear stopped, dropped to his knees in front of the fellow, and prayed, "Lord thank you for this meal I'm about to receive." —*Boyce G.*

The Hail Storm

I was driving in North Augusta when suddenly there came up a hailstorm. It was like thousands of baseballs hitting the car at the same time. I was scared and didn't know what to do. I tried to get under an overpass, but everyone else had thought of that before me. So, I called my husband Tommy on my cell phone and asked him what to do.

    He said, "Get the hell out of there!"

    Pealey later asked me, "Will you call Tommy the next time you're in a hailstorm?"

    I replied, "The hell I will!" —*Winkey M.*

Baptizing Rooster

Cousin Earl, a Baptist Preacher at Little Horse Creek Baptist Church, was going to baptize "Rooster," a notoriously mean, drunken, no-good son-of-a-gun. Rooster was Earl's oldest sister's husband, and after Earl's mother died when he was about nine years old, he had to live with his sister and Rooster.

Rooster would come home drunk and beat Earl and his brother just for the fun of it. He was a mean man! After Rooster got old and was close to death, he accepted the Lord and asked Earl to baptize him.

The baptizing was set for Sunday service, but Earl forgot to heat the water in the baptismal pool! When Ole Rooster stepped into that freezing water it took his breath away, it was so cold.

Everyone knew that he wanted to cuss up a storm, but he did not dare! Sister Sue (a member of the church) was there and watched Ole Rooster come to the Lord. Sue later told Earl she thought he did that on purpose.
—*Juli C.*

Note: To show how mean Rooster was, at one point the KKK sent Rooster a message. They burned a cross in his front yard! He moved his family to Augusta, Georgia.

Cussing

I was about five years old when my grandpa took me down to where my Pa was working on a house (Pa was a carpenter). I heard Pa say something about "puttin that damn floor in." After I got home, Grandma asked me what my Daddy was doing and I said, "Puttin in a damn floor." Grandma beat the living daylights out of me for cussing. She felt bad after she found out I was just repeating what my Daddy said. —*Francis G.*

"Do not worry about your children not listening to you. They do, and then you punish them for it." —*Juli C.*

Baptizing Carl

Earl and I were getting ready to baptize Brother Carl. Carl was a dwarf and was quite heavy, and it took the two of us to do it. I said to Earl, "Since Carl is so old [about forty], maybe we should hold him under a little longer to make sure it takes." Carl did not think that was funny. —*Bobby L.*

Eco-Friendly

Today, we girls went out to lunch and after we ate, we were talking about babies. Someone mentioned something about washing diapers. Erin popped up and said, "I'm not giving up disposable diapers, I'll be eco-friendly later and plant a tree!" We all agreed that she needed to plant a whole grove. —*Juli C.*

Nasal Congestion

We girls were out to lunch—Sue, Pealey, Winkey, Erin, Morgan, baby Emily, and me. Pealey stated that every time she comes down here from Charlotte, her nose gets stuffed-up. Morgan (five years old) did not understand what "stuffed-up" meant. Erin explained to her that Aunt Pealey's nose was congested. Morgan came around the table and got in Pealey's face and said, "You're not stuffed-up; you just got boogers in your nose!" Erin was mortified. —*Juli C.*

Morgan & Emily

Ma Bailing Out

I was taking Daddy to the doctor; Mamma was in the car with us. The old car started to overheat, and steam was coming from under the hood. Ma hollered, "Stop this car and let me out."

I said, "Hold on," but Ma started opening the back door.

Pa said, "A-n-n-n-t!"

Ma said, "A-n-n-n-t my foot, I'm getting out!"
—*Ned B.*

"Lord put your arm around my shoulder and your hand over my mouth." —*Old Saying*

Cracking Windows

While living in New York City, I worked for my husband's uncle who owned a garment factory. Well, it was summertime and hot as Hades. There was no air-conditioning, not even a fan. I said to no one in particular, "I'm going to crack some windows."

Uncle Rogie looked at me and said, "You do, and I'll crack your head." Up north they had never heard this expression for opening a window. —*Juli C.*

Class Reunion

I went to my ten-year class reunion in Pohokee, Florida. Everyone took turns getting up and telling what they had done with their lives. When it was my turn, I got up and said, "Well, my family moved back to South Carolina, and I became a brain surgeon." I sat down and looked over at my husband Ralph. He had this surprised look on his face. That was the biggest story he had ever heard me tell! —*Twiddle J.*

Donnie and Ned

A lady at church told me that she had seen Donnie and that he looked just like Ned. I said, "That was Ned" and the woman said, "No it was Donnie!"

And I said, "Donnie is Ned," but she still argued with me. It took a while to convince her that Donnie and Ned are the same person.

It is confusing. There are so many of us and we all have nick names. —*Lottie G. (a.k.a., Sue, Suzie Q, Susie)*

Ned & Deana

When Pigs Fly or Stumble

When Mickey and Joey were teenagers, their Daddy told them to take the corn mash (leftovers from a little moonshine making) and to feed it to the hogs." Now boys, just give them a little at a time every day." Well, the boys thought it over and decided to feed it to them all at once (the boys had been going to the movies on their minds and wanted to get their chores over with). So, they fed them all the mash at once.

Well, those hogs got as high as a Georgia pine, and when Chester saw what they had done, he got mad! "Boys, you two have killed my hogs!" Those hogs were stumbling and falling all over the place; it looked like a valley drunks convention!

Well, the boys had to pay for their misdeed. Chester made them tear down the hog fence and then put it up again.

While putting up the fence, Mickey started complaining, so Chester kicked him in the rump and sent him flying! Mickey said he never complained again where his Daddy could hear him. —*Pealey H.*

"Never take down a fence until you know why it was put up in the first place."
—*J. F. Kennedy*

"I saw that!"
—*God*

Thunderstorms in the Morning

The Busbee family has been having a picnic at Easter sense Lottie was a baby. She was born in 1939, so it has been eighty plus years of carrying on this tradition. We always had our picnic on Easter Sunday until 1991. Deana had come all the way from Knoxville, Tennessee, and had to leave Sunday afternoon to go to work on Monday. Well, her son Jordan missed the Easter egg hunt and cried all the way home. When I told Mama about it, she decided we would start having our picnic on the Saturday before Easter.

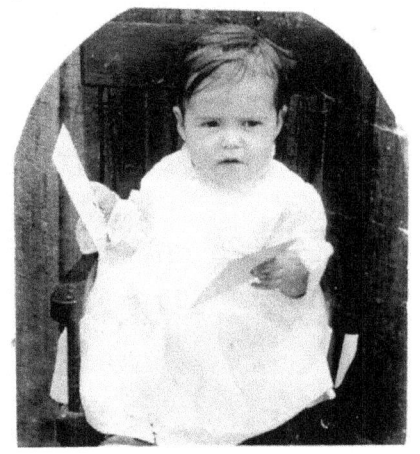

Nora Leopard Busbee

One year I came home for Easter. I was living in Nashville at the time.

Well, we got up that Saturday morning and it was storming! I said to Mama, "What are we going to do? We have over a hundred people coming."

Mama said, "Don't worry, a storm in the morning is like an old woman dancing. It won't last long."

And she was right! By eleven o'clock the sun came out and it was a wonderful day. —*Juli C.*

Tying Knots

I had pulled out a piece of ribbon to tie around the neck of the stuffed animal that GiGi was carrying around "to fancy it up." I asked her if she knew how to tie a bow, she said, "No, all I can tie is knots." —*Deana W.*

Mistaken Identity

Back in the sixties, Ken was little, and I took him to a store in Aiken to buy him a pair of shoes. After a few days, the shoes started coming apart. I took the shoes back and asked for another pair. The shop owner did not want to exchange them. Well, I raised a ruckus and got my money back. A few days later my sister Twiddle went shopping in the same store and when the owner saw her, he thought it was me and asked her to leave, saying he did not want her business. The owner also went to the Bank where my husband was the manager and told him he did not want me in his store again! Poor Twiddle did not have a clue. —*Juli C.*

The Big Game

Blake's big soccer game. Blake scored twice for his team, once for the other team and then he knocked himself out when he ran into the goal post!
—*Granny Winkey*

Health Insurance

Mama was in St. Joseph's Hospital in Augusta, Georgia. My sister Twiddle and I heard that an old schoolmate of ours—Clyde—was in the same hospital, so we decided to have some fun. We got some surgical masks, clipboards, and paper, put on the masks, and went into his room. His wife and minister were there. We told him we were from the hospital finance office, that his insurance would not cover his bill, and that he had to pay up that day in cash or leave! Of course, Clyde got upset. I wish you could have seen the look on his face. Well, what we did not know was that Clyde had a bad heart! We felt bad after we found this out, and Clyde swore he would get even with us. —*Winkey M.*

Movie Stars

Mr. B and I were talking about movie stars. Mr. B talked about how beautiful the female stars were back in the fifties. He looked at me and said, "And you have nice eyebrows." I am sure he had to think long and hard to come up with something pretty about me. —*Twiddle J.*

Cremating Rik

For years Rik liked to boast about how when he died, he wanted to be cremated and his ashes put in a cannon and shot out over the Stones River Battlefield in Murfreesboro, Tennessee. I had listened to this for years and was sick of hearing it. One night he was pretty tipsy, and he said, "It's now official. I've put it in my will that if my wishes aren't followed about being cremated and my ashes shot out of a cannon over the Stones River Battlefield, then no one will share in my estate."

    I looked at him and said, "Oh I'll have you cremated alright, then I'm going to flush your a-- down the toilet!" For once in that man's life, he was speechless.
—*Juli C.*

The Pap Test

Forty-something years ago while I was getting a pap test, the doctor came in, got himself settled on his stool, looked at me, and said, "My what a beautiful . . ." Then he caught himself and said, "What a beautiful tan line you have!" You should have seen the look on the nurse's face! —*Twiddle J.*

Mr. Johnson's Car

It was back in the late sixties. Ralph had a new Mustang. His dad and mom were taking a trip out west and asked to use Ralph's new car. Mr. Johnson left his old car behind for us to use while they were out west. Ralph worked in the mill at night. One day I was coming home from Lottie's and driving Mr. Johnson's old car, and I reached over to take the blanket off the baby's face. When I did, I must have turned the steering wheel because I ran into a fence and messed up the side of the car.

Well, I went back to Lottie's and asked her to help me beat the dents out. We both got hammers and started to work; it did not take long to see that we were making it worse! Now the paint was peeling off where we beat the dents. I took the car home and parked it where you could not see the damage. Ralph drove his dad's old car to work every day and never saw where it was messed up.

About a month later Mr. Johnson came home, pulled into the yard and the first thing he saw was his dentedup car. He got out and said, "Damn, Ralph! What did you do to my car?"

I eased on into the house like I did not know anything. The funny thing was Mr. Johnson hauled a trailer behind Ralph's car and had installed big old mirrors to the side of that new Mustang!
—*Twiddle J.*

Aiken's Makings, September 2009

At Aiken's annual craft show there was a booth with paintings that were wonderful. They were all lambs, they were cute, and each had a title. After reading the titles, the paintings made sense and were so funny. One was a lamb taped to a wall with duct tape. It also had duct tape over the lamb's mouth and the caption read, "Silence of the Lamb." Another was a lamb pulling a donkey on a board that had wheels. The caption read, "Hauling Ass." Sue, Katie, and I spent more than half an hour reading and laughing at those paintings. That was the most fun I had had in years. —*Juli C.*

"Never say never unless you like the taste of Crow!" —*Juli C.*

Condos at School

Ralph, Twiddle, Mickey, and I were sitting around talking, and Ralph started talking about condominiums. I guess Twiddle was not half listening and she replied, "Yeah I hear that they're giving them out at schools." She thought Ralph had said "condoms." Now, every time I hear the word "condos" I start laughing.
—*Pealey H.*

On The Road with Bobby and Betty

Bobby and Betty were on the road with their RV. Bobby pulled into a rest stop to use the restroom. Betty said she did not need to go and stayed in the RV. After Bobby left, Betty changed her mind and went to the lady's room. Bobby came out and, thinking Betty was in the RV, took off. Betty saw him drive off. She borrowed someone's cell phone and called Bobby and said, "Come back and get me."

Bobby said, "Stop fooling around."

Then Betty said, "I'm not fooling. Come back and get me!" He finally pulled over and checked; sure enough, he had left Betty at the rest stop!

—*Ralph J.*

"Sometimes when I open my mouth my mother comes out." —*Old Saying*

Going Potty

While visiting Deana at Christmas in 2010, Jordan's girlfriend was there with her two-year-old GiAnna. She followed Deana into the bathroom. While Deana was on the toilet, GiAnna patted her on the leg and said, "Push, Grandma, push," and made a nose as if pushing. When Deana, finished GiAnna said, "Good girl Grandma, you did potty." She put up her hand and said, "High five." —*Juli C.*

Wally World

When I was little, I thought that "Wally World" was a theme park. —*Leah C., eleven years old*

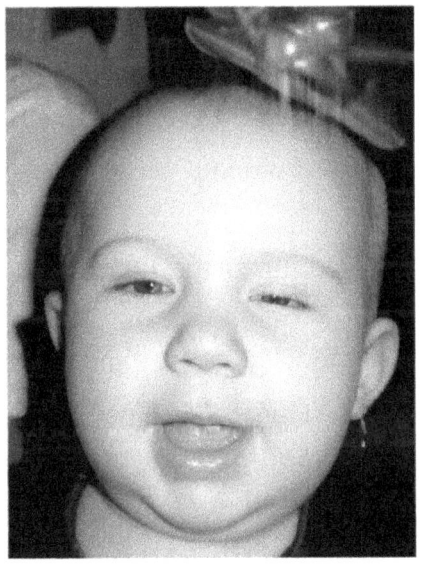

Leah Carrera

The Devil

While visiting Ken in Florida, we were going to see five-year-old Leah's artwork, which was being displayed at the community center. Ken stopped to get gas while Laura, Pealey, Leah, and I sat in the SUV. Leah started looking up. I asked what she was doing, and she said, "I'm looking at heaven."

Then she looked down and I asked, "What are you doing now?"

She said, "I'm looking at the Devil."

I said, "You know that sometimes the Devil gets into people and makes them do bad things."

Leah said, "Yeah, he got in Mama one time."

Laura jumped in and said, "No he did not! But he may have influenced me a couple of times." Well, Pealey and I started laughing and could not stop.
—*Grandma Juli*

Applying For a Job

Ned went to apply for a job and the interviewer asked him, "Well what do you think you're worth?"
 Ned said, "Man I've got to have more than that."
—*Robert B.*

Robbing Honey

We had all gone to Aunt Fannie's house for Sunday dinner (this was about 1947). Daddy, Mama, Uncle Lonnie, Lonnie's wife Lucille, and all of us kids were there. On the way home, Lonnie tells Daddy that he knows where there is a tree with a honeybee's nest in it in Bath. Well, they decide to rob that nest on the way home. (I am sure that this was Uncle Lonnie idea.) They tell the women to stay in the car. They parked away from the tree. Well, Aunt Lucille decided she would see how they robbed the nest. Suddenly, she hollered out, "The son-of-a-B---- pinched me!" Lucille was from Belgium; Lonnie married her while he was in Europe during WWII. The only English she knew when she came to America were cuss words that she learned from Uncle Lonnie. —*Lottie G.*

Fat Feet

Mama was in the hospital. The nurse was checking her ankles and said, "Mrs. Busbee, your ankles are swollen."

Mama laughed and said, "No honey, that's just fat that has settled down around my feet." —*Lottie G.*

Easter, Early 1990s

We were having our Easter picnic at Carl's house; there were more than a hundred people there. While we were eating, a black man came to the fence and said he was hungry. Carl asked me to fix him a plate, so I did, and Carl gave it to the man. Carl turned to say something to one of the kids and when he turned back, the man had disappeared! Carl was baffled. He looked for the man, but the man was gone! Later Carl told me he thought the man was an angel that God had sent to test us. I think he was right. Carl died at age fifty. I miss him. —*Juli C.*

Carl & Rusty

Old Sayings

Gayle was here visiting this weekend. She is doing research on her Scottish ancestors, so we drove up to Bethune, South Carolina (northeast of Camden). We found the cemetery where her ancestors are buried. I said to her, "Then you're a South Carolinian."

She replied, "Yeah, I bet my great-great-grandpa's rabbit ran through your great-great-grandpa's collard patch!"

I love old sayings. —*Juli C.*

Duct Tape

While Gayle and I were in Camden, South Carolina, we stopped at a historical site where they had a welcome center and gift shop. The director of the site was very friendly and told us this story:

An iron worker in Historic Williamsburg, Virginia, was making nails. A man and his wife were watching, and the woman said, "That's not period; they didn't have nails during colonial days."
   The worker said, "Yeah, I guess that they used duct tape to hang Jesus to the cross!" —*Juli C.*

Spelling Test

When Leah was six and a half years old, she asked for paper and pencils. I asked what she needed them for, and she said, "I'm giving Baby Gi a spelling test." Baby Gi was not even three years old." Baby Gi failed the test!" Leah said, "She just scribbled on the paper."
—*Grandma Juli*

"Pull your big girl panties up and deal with it!"
—*Anonymous*

Bad Cookies

One day this man from church came to visit Mickey. I had just finished making some Christmas ornaments out of salt and flour that looked like cookies. The man asked if he could have one of those cookies and Mickey said, "Yeah, Pealey won't mind."

The man took a bite and tried to chew it, he spit it out and said, "Man! That is the worst thing I have ever tasted!" That man never let me forget about those bad cookies. —*Pealey H.*

Mentally Challenged

We were talking about a man who was mentally challenged, and I said, "His elevator doesn't go all the way to the top."

Pealey said, "He's one brick shy of a full load."

Sue said, "His dipstick doesn't go all the way to the bottom."

Someone else said, "He didn't have both oars in the water, and he's not the sharpest knife in the drawer."

I love old sayings. —*Juli C.*

Lazy or Just Plain Dumb

Daddy told me this. When he was a young man, they had some neighbors who were really lazy. They were too lazy to cut wood to heat the house, so they started tearing the boards off the side of the house to burn in the stove. He remembers seeing them walking around in the house and all you could see were their legs because they were working their way from the bottom to the top. —*Robert B.*

Dental Work

Pealey and I were talking about having dental work done. She said, "I have sixteen crowns; my husband always said that he had a "Caddy" in my mouth!"
—*Juli C.*

"Of course, I talk to myself. Sometimes I need expert advice." —*Juli C.*

On The Clock

Pealey and I were visiting Ken in Florida. He was fussing at Leah about doing her homework. Leah looked at him and said, "Aren't you supposed to be working, you're still on the clock." (Ken worked from home.) I guess he is always telling her he is on the clock.
—*Grandma Juli*

Mad Hen

Today, Pealey and I drove Sue to Augusta to buy an antique bed. On the way home we stopped at Harrison's hardware store to get some lag bolts for the bed. I went in to get someone to come out and look at the bed to see what size bolts we needed. In the meantime, this man drives up in a truck and tells the man helping us to have Wayne come out and get his chicken out of the back of his truck. Wayne came out, got the hen and three eggs out of the bed of the truck, then put the hen down and went back inside. Well, the hen started walking around squawking. She was mad! Then she jumped up on the hood of a new truck and was raising a ruckus. Only in a small town! —*Juli C.*

Favorite Sayings

"May all your children be born naked!"
—Mickey

"Put that in your pipe and smoke it!"
—Mickey

"Well, Jimmy crack corn and I do not care."
—Twiddle

"What in the wide world of sports was that!"
—Robert

"Poppy cock, you say!"
—Juli

Fish Story

My brother Don went fishing on Lake Murray, filled his boat with fish (the limit), took them home, emptied them, then came back and caught another boatload. A man stopped by and asked how it was going. Don told him about all the fish he had caught.

The man asked, "Do you know who I am?"

Don said, "No."

The man said, "I am the Game warden! And you have caught more than the limit."

Don said, "Do you know who I am?"

The man said "No."

Don said, "I'm the biggest liar in Greenwood County." —*Helen H.*

Guard Dog

Glen came home drunk one night, and our dog would not let him into the house. Every time he got close, the dog would bite him. In fact, the dog chased him down to the back of our property and kept him there the rest of the night. —*Marty L.*

Peace in the Middle East

Me, Ned, Uncle Euman, and Pa were talking about the war in the Middle East. Pa said, "If they want to end that war, all they have to do is give John D. a sack of tools, set him behind the enemy line, and let him work on their equipment." —*Robert B.*

Women in War

Mrs. Lottie Byrd always said that women could not fight a war because when one stopped to go to the bathroom, they would all have to go! —*Lottie G.*

"Twiddle dresses to kill, she also cooks that way." —*Ralph J.*

The Day Aunt Pealey Moved

It was raining the morning Aunt Pealey was going to move (March 31st). Kyle said, "April showers came a day early this year." —*Katie W.*

Remembering Numbers

Me and Kyle were in my truck helping move Pealey and when we got to the gate at the storage place, there was a keypad. We had to punch in a code. I asked Kyle if he remembered the number and Kyle replied, "You're asking a guy with a brain tumor to remember numbers!" —*Robert B.*

Eyebrows

During Easter Saturday picnic at Johnny's house, a group of us women were sitting around outside talking, when Pealey came over and said, "Well I found my eyebrows. They were hiding under my arms." She has lost her eyebrows. Most of mine are gone, too, so I just draw mine on. I guess my artistic talents come in handy.
—*Juli C.*

Two Fingers

My friend Jean has a sister named Helen, and they have this system; if either of them is repeating something, the other will hold up two fingers. Well, I had told Sister Twiddle about this. So, the first time Twiddle met Jean, Jean started to say something, and Twiddle held up two fingers. Well Jean was so surprised that she forgot what she was going to say. She knew that the two-finger thing was something that only her sister Helen knew about! And besides, she had never even met Twiddle!
—*Pealey H.*

While I am talking on the phone with someone I will say, "If I'm repeating myself hold up two fingers."
—*Juli C.*

Hostage Cookbook

We were at the hospital visiting Sister Sue after she fell on her back steps and broke her ankle. It was Pealey, Marty, and me. We were talking, and Marty asked if anyone had an extra family cookbook. Her son Neil had gotten a divorce and his ex-wife was holding his cookbook hostage. —*Juli C.*

Shaved or Bathed

My friend Jewel sent her husband to the groomers to have their two cats bathed. He dropped them off and later went back to pick them up. The groomer had shaved the male cat! There was not a hair left on him! When he got home, the male cat was in shock and each time the female looked at him, she would bow up and hiss. Well, Jewel was enraged.

Louie said, "Now Jewel don't be upset. It was probably my fault, so take your anger out on me."

And she did!

Louie is from Ireland and still has a heavy accent. He could have said "bathe," and the groomer thought he said "shave." —*Juli C.*

Can't Remember

My ankle was broken, and I had a hard time walking. I needed to go to the bathroom, so I hobbled in, combed my hair, then hobbled back to the living room and sat down. Then I remembered why I had gone in there in the first place! —*Lottie G.*

Technology

I needed to call Winkey, so I walked over to the microwave and punched in her number and waited for her to answer! —*Twiddle J.*

Twiddle

New Mexico

In New Mexico, it is so flat that if your dog runs away from home, you can watch him for three days.
—*Marc W.*

Public Speaking

Today I gave a talk to the St. Thaddeus Church Women's Lunch Bunch. I talked about women in history and what inspired them, then I talked about my paintings and what inspired me. Tonight, Sister Sue asked me how it went, and I replied, "Very well. No one got up and left, and only one lady fell asleep!" —*Juli C.*

Flirting

When Jewell and I were teenagers, I loved to flirt. Grandpa would park his taxi across the street from where I worked in Aiken, and I would whistle at him. He told me to stop that because all men had dog in them! I suppose he was worried about men passing by getting the wrong idea about me. His friends would tease him about a young girl flirting with him.
—*Lottie G.*

Martintown Road

Back during the Civil War, a family named Martin lived in what is now North Augusta. The men of the family had gone off to fight, so the women of the family ran the farm. They had heard that a Union courier was coming through, so the women dressed in men's clothing, hid out along the road, and attacked the courier. They did not kill him. They just roughed him up really good and took his sack of communications, then rushed back home and changed clothes. Later that evening, the courier came staggering up to their door and told the story about a gang of men who beat him up and took his sack. He never knew that his attackers were women! —*Katie W.*

Kyle, Mollie, Katie, Marc

Mama Didn't Like Strom Thurman

When Mama was in her seventies and complained about being tired, I would say, "Look at Strom Thurman. He's twenty years older than you, and he's still working."
 Mama would get mad and say, "That man never worked a day in his life." —*Lottie G.*

College Education

Ms. Yvonne's neighbor's son was graduating from college, and she sent him a gift. The young man wrote her a thank you note using six words. He misspelled three! —*Pealey H.*

Storing Junk

I had been wanting to get a storage building for some time and Billy finally said, "Go ahead and get one, but don't go putting a lot of junk in there!" —*Lottie G.*

Lucky

I saw this article in the paper about a missing dog; he was described as blind in one eye, deaf, had three legs, and answered to the name of "Lucky." —*Lottie G.*

Last Chance

Summer has a dog, which she found on the side of the road. He had been hit by a car and was in bad shape. She took him to the vet, and they had to amputate one of his back legs, so she named him Last Chance!
—*Juli C.*

Laundering Money

I wanted to hide some money, so I decided to put it in the bottom of the laundry bin. I thought to myself, I guess I'm laundering money. —*Kelley W.*

Bragging

I had been talking to my cousin Diane and she said, "You have accomplished so much in your life. Does your family know all that you have done?"

I said "No."

She asked, "Why not?"

I said, "My family don't take well to bragging. You try it, and they will cut you off at the knees."

Later that day I was telling this to some family members who stopped by to visit (Katie, Marc, Kyle, and Robert). Kyle popped up and said, "Yeah, then you wouldn't have a leg to stand on!" I love Kyle. —*Juli C.*

I Believe

Tommy and I were watching TV with our grandson Micah, and there was a commercial showing Santa. Micah (ten years old) said, "That is just a costume. I know all about that."

I said, "Have you told your little brother?"

He said, "No."

I said, "Tell your Poppop what you just told me."

He did and Tommy said, "Well if you believe, you get lots of gifts, but if you don't believe, you don't get anything."

Micah sat up and instantly said, "I believe!"

—*Granny Winkey*

Foul Language

I went to a ballgame with Twiddle and Ralph. Their great-grandson Will was playing. Will's other great-grandmother was there, and she was yelling at Will, telling him what to do. She was using foul language. When she realized what she had said, she looked at me and said, "Excuse my French."

I replied, "That didn't sound like French to me. It sounded like Valley." —*Pealey H.*

The Cure

We were at Brother John's house for breakfast the day after Thanksgiving. Ken, Winkey, Twiddle, and I were doing the dishes and talking about the medicine that Mama gave us when we were kids. Twiddle told about the strong black coffee Mama would put castor oil in one half cup coffee and one-half cup Castor oil. That was her remedy for whatever ailed you. Yeah, I was supposed to have long blond silky hair, be five-foot-nine-inches tall with flawless complexion, and have an hourglass figure. Just look at what the remedy did to me!" Twiddle has dark hair, is about five feet tall, and weighs about one hundred pounds. —*Juli C.*

Googling

Ralph had been getting a lot of calls from telemarketers. One day a man called and said that Ralph had a problem with his computer. Ralph said, "Oh yeah?"

The man said, "If you will just follow my instructions, I'll fix it for you."

Ralph said, "Okay."

The man said, "Now turn on your computer."

Ralph J.

Ralph said, "Okay, it's on."

The man said, "Now just do what I tell you, "and he told Ralph to hit certain keys.

Ralph said, "Okay, now I'm Googling?"

The man got agitated and said, "No, no, don't Google."

Ralph kept this up until the man hung up on him! Ralph does not have a computer! —*Twiddle J.*

"Someone said that they had googled me; I asked, "How did it feel?" —*Juli C.*

When asked which one of us Busbee women was the oldest, Twiddle said, "She won't admit it, but I think its Mama."

In Style

Twiddle saw a young man walking along the side of the road. He had on the stylish pants that young men wear. They were hanging below his cheeks with his underwear showing, the crotch was below his knees, and he was using one hand in front and one hand in back to hold them up as he walked. Twiddle said, "I wish I had had a slingshot. I would have popped him good!" —*Pealey H.*

Uninsured Redneck

I was sitting in a fast-food restaurant after church one Sunday. Looking out the window, I saw this car drive by and had a chuckle. It was a sporty hatchback with duct tape going crosswise from the front of the roof to the back bumper. I thought to myself, there goes an uninsured redneck! Ah-h-h the wonder of duct tape!
—*Juli C.*

Friendly Fly

Genny and George were visiting a church on Jekyll Island, Georgia. During the service this fly kept buzzing their heads. Later Genny told George, "That fly was the friendliest thing in that church!" —*Juli C.*

Pa Hauling Guiana

Back in 1976 I was living out in the country about fourteen miles from Aiken in Rocky Springs. Pa had come out to get a load of chicken manure from a farmer. While he was out there, he decided to visit me. Mama was with him. When they passed Mr. Frank Quattlebaum's house, Mr. Frank saw him (when you live in the country you notice when a vehicle passes, as it may be the only one you see all day).

Pa & Boys, 1976

On the way home, Pa went through Aiken and had gotten to the top of Kalmir Hill when Mama looked back and said to Pa, "Where's your trailer?" Pa looked back. Sure enough, it was gone! In the meantime, Mr. Frank called me and said that Pa's load of manure was in front of his house, and he wanted me to come get it! It was late summer, and it smelled bad. I told him Pa would come back for it, and he did. —*Pealey H.*

Flash Cards

Four-year-old Silas was being tested at school, and the lady doing the testing was using "flash cards." After a while Silas said, "Can we play another game? I am tired of this one." —*Granny Katie*

Restriction

It was Katie's birthday, and we sisters had gone out to lunch. Marty had brought her granddaughter Sam with her because she was on restriction. We talked about how now-a-days kids get punished with a time out or restriction or taking away their cell phones and personal computers. When we were kids, we did not get restrictions. We got a stick on our behinds. Marty said, "Yeah, the only thing I wish that Mama had taken away from me was that hoe!" (We grew up on a farm.)
—*Juli C.*

Going Deaf

When we were little, Mama started losing her hearing. Daddy went to bed early every night at 8:00 PM, even in the summertime before the sun went down. We all had to go to bed except Mama; she would stay up and read. Every ten to fifteen minutes, she would holler out, "Alright, y'all go to sleep. You're going to wake up your Daddy!" We were being quiet. *Mama* was the one keeping him awake. —*Marty L.*

"Boney Grandma was a cross between Olive Oil and Granny Clampett." —*Marty L.*

Picking Peas

We were all in the pea field up from the house, me, Katie, Robert, Carl, Ned, and Mama. Mama would come along to keep the boys from fighting. Well, we had finished picking peas and had loaded them on the trailer that was hitched to the tractor. Usually, Robert was the only one allowed to drive the tractor, but this time Ned decided he was driving. We all piled on the trailer and Ned started down the hill. He was going too fast and took the curve too sharply and threw all of us and the peas off the trailer! When Mama got up off the ground that little heifer was some kind of mad!
—*Marty L.*

Ned aggravating Mama

"Yeah, she made us all walk home." —*Katie W.*

Fussing

Have you ever opened your mouth and words come out before filtering through your brain? That is what happened to me when I was about fourteen years old. Mama had been fussing all morning long, and I had had enough! I said, "Why don't you just go ahead and beat me and stop fussing." Well, she backhanded me across the face and when I got up off the floor, I decided I would not ever say that again! Mama kept on fussing.
—Juli C.

Dancing In Church

There was an article in the paper about this old building in Kitching Mill that was a library. Plans were to move it to Aiken and turn it into a museum. They interviewed this old black woman who said at one time the building had been a church and she had been kicked out of the church for dancing. She said, "I had the Lord in my heart but the devil in my feet!" —*Lottie G.*

Staying on Restriction

While Mandy was in high school, I called one Saturday and Mandy answered the phone. I asked, "What are you doing home on a Saturday?"

She said, "I'm on restriction."

A couple of months later I called to talk to Robert, and Mandy answered the phone, so I asked, "Are you on restriction again?"

She replied, "I've never gotten off!"

Mandy B.

Her Mom Reba was telling a neighbor about Mandy being on restriction so long and the neighbor asked, "What did she do, kill somebody?" Poor Mandy.
—Juli C.

Getting Old

"First you forget names, then you forget faces, then you forget to pull your zipper up, then you forget to pull your zipper down!"
—*Leo Rosenberg*

Dottie West Look-a-Like

Back in the early nineties, I was living in Nashville and apparently, I looked a lot like Dottie West (the country singer). One night, my husband and I had had dinner at the Stockyard, **the** place to go to hear and see country stars. When we had finished dinner, we were going downstairs to the night club and people were coming up the stairs. Well, this man thought I was Dottie. He grabbed my hand and babbled on about what a great singer I was. I did not have the heart to tell him he had made a mistake! —*Juli C.*

Juli C.

"There is many a great tune played on an old fiddle." —*Old saying*

"If the young only knew; if the old only could."
—*French saying*

The Gas Tank

In 1969, Ken was three years old. He loved his tricycle and would park it behind my car in the carport. One morning I was taking Deana to school. I walked around the front of the car and got in, backed up, and heard this scraping noise. I stopped, got out and looked and I had backed over Ken's tricycle and the handlebar had punched a hole in the gas tank! That night when Joe came home, I told him about it. He was not happy. He had it repaired, which cost $100, which was a lot of money back then. Two weeks later, Ken parked his tricycle behind my car, and I backed over it again! I put another hole in the gas tank! Joe got so mad he beat that tricycle up and threw it in the garbage. Ken did not have wheels again until he was big enough for a bicycle.
—Juli C.

Women's Lib

Feb. 27, 2013: I just talked to Deana today, and I was telling her about a show I had watched on TV last night. It was about "women's lib." I commented that it started back in the sixties and about how much better it is now than it was back then, and she said, *"Yeah, it's Kelley's turn to cook tonight, which means we're going out to eat."*
—*Juli C.*

A Bad Day In Prosperity

Pealey and I were in Irmo, South Carolina. I was visiting her up at the lake, and we stopped at a hamburger place to have lunch. I had my little dog Savannah with me and left her in the car. After we ate and went back out to the car, Pealey looked for her keys and could not find them. She had locked them in the car with the dog! While trying to decide what to do, we saw a locksmith shop across the street, so Pealey walked over and asked for help. A man came over and unlocked the door. While working, he asked Pealey, "What year is it?"

Pealey said, "It's 1995!"

He said, "No, what year is the car?" He charged $50 to unlock it.

Later Pealey was telling her husband Mickey about what had happened he said, "Why didn't you use the hide-a-key under the car?" —*Juli C.*

"Be yourself," is about the worst advice you can give some people! —*Tom Masson*

"A good scare is worth more to a man than good advice!" —*Edgar Watson Howe*

Growing His Flock

The Priest at All Saints Episcopal Church in Beech Island was trying to grow his flock, so he went out and did some cold calling, inviting everyone to come to church. He went to James Brown's house and invited him. The following Sunday, James showed up at the church and told the priest that he could not stay but wanted to contribute. He pulled out a roll of cash big enough to choke a horse and peeled off a few large bills, gave them to the priest, and left. —*Barney L.*

The Tip

While my niece was in college, she worked as a waitress at a restaurant in Southside. Late one night, James Brown's chauffeur came in to get a cup of coffee and a snack for James. A few minutes later he came back in with a $10 tip! That was back in the sixties, so $10 was a lot of money. —*Ellie C.*

Wisdom

"Do not use a chain saw when a butter knife will do." —*Juli C.*

Blue Footed Boobies

I said to Twiddle, "Don't tell me that God doesn't have a sense of humor. Look at the blue footed Booby." This is a bird with blue feet. Twiddle said, "Yeah, look at Al Sharpton!" —*Juli C.*

Gratitude

I was in a very depressed state. Life had beaten me down. I called my friend Marilyn and after she listened to me moan and groan, she told me to make a list of four things for which I was grateful. That night I tried to make a list, but nothing would come. The next morning, I called Marilyn and told her I could not come up with four things. I could only think of two. She asked what they were, and I said, "I'm not pregnant and I have beer in the refrigerator." —*Gayle C.*

Dead Cat

I read this in the paper. A little boy's cat died while he was at school. His mom agonized over how to tell him, so she finally decided to tell him as gently as she could. She said, "I'm sorry to tell you but your cat has died and has gone to heaven."

Her son looked at her and said, "Why would God want a dead cat?" —*Twiddle J.*

Come to Jesus Meeting

It has been a cold hard winter in 2014. We had temperatures in the single digits in January. February 12th there was an ice storm (three to four inches), and my power was off for five days. It looked like a tornado had come through the south. On Feb. 15th we had an earthquake, 4.1 on the Richter scale. The next day we had aftershocks. I was talking to my sister about all this bad weather, and she said, "Someone must have ticked God off."

And I said, "Yeah, and I think we have just had a Come to Jesus Meeting." —*Juli C.*

Life Decisions

My friend and I were talking on the phone (she was in her car on her cell phone), and we were talking about what she could do to keep busy after she retires in six months. I suggested she do the things she loves, like traveling and giving speeches (she is so at ease with public speaking). She answered, "But can I make a living at that?"

I replied, "Well if that doesn't work out you can always take up prostitution."

She laughed so hard she ran off the road. At church the next day, I was talking to this elderly lady in her nineties. We talked about living a long life, and she said in order to live a long life you needed to laugh. That reminded me about my friend, so I told her the story. She laughed along with me and said, "Yeah she could be sitting on a gold mine!" I just had to call my friend to tell her what Ms. Eloise had said. —*Juli C.*

Twitter Button

I said to Josh, "Show me where the button is on the keyboard for Twitter. I cannot find that little bird emblem."

Josh said, "Mama, you need to stick to your accounting program." —*Marty L.*

"And may the bird of paradise fly up your nose." —*Mickey H.*

Dumb Thief

This man broke into a house and stole some bonds. He tried to cash them but could not because you need an ID, so he went back, broke in again and left a note saying he would give the bonds back for money. He left his phone number! —*Winkey M.*

Full Tick

Pealey, Winkey, and I had gone out for lunch and when I dropped Winkey off at her house she said, "Whew - I'm as stuffed as a full tick on a skinny dog." —*Juli C.*

Buzzards

It was a Sunday morning, and Kelley and I were going to Leipers Fork (a town outside Nashville) for breakfast. We had gone through a bad storm after we left the house. While we were driving, I looked out the window and saw about a dozen buzzards on a big electric tower, with their wings spread out. I said to Kelley, "Oh my God, they've been electrocuted!"

He laughed at me and said, "I think they're just drying their wings." —*Deana C.*

Deana C.

"Well Butter my buns and call me a biscuit."
—*Anonymous*

Bad Haircut

Kelley decided to give himself a haircut, and he used his electric razor. He gapped it up here and there, then he tried to correct it. The more he cut, the worse it got. He finally put his cap on and went to the barber shop. When he took his cap off the men in the shop laughed at him and said, "A do-it-yourself job, eah?"
—*Deana W.*

Summer of '75

Johnny and Daddy were sitting in the yard and talking. Someone had dropped off a dog, and he kept going back and forth across the road. Johnny was afraid it would get run over so he got a stick and went and beat the dog and told it to stay out of the road. He came back and sat on a log that was turned upright. John David (three years old) came up behind Johnny and hit him across the back with a broom handle and said, "Now, how dat feel to you!" —*Lottie G.*

John David

All of a sudden, the lights went out! and then I felt this intense pain in my back. —*Johnny B.*

The Gift

It was Morgan's birthday, and a woman brought her little girl to the party. She brought both Morgan and little sister Emmy a gift. Mom Erin said to Emmy, "What do you say?"

Emmy said, "I don't like it!" Well, Erin was so embarrassed; I have never seen her so mad.
—*Granny Winkey*

Answered Prayer

Sue met me over at my rental house. My renter had moved out and had left five old tires and a box so large it took both of us to lift it. The box was full of trash. Sue had brought her old truck so we could haul all this stuff to the landfill. We put the box of trash in first, next a big Christmas tree, next the tires (one was really heavy), and we packed the smaller stuff where we could. I said to Sue, "Remember the last time we hauled stuff to the landfill? We did not get to the top of the hill before we lost a big piece of red carpet."

Sue laughed and said, *"Yeah I remember."* Sue told me to drive and handed me the keys.

I got in the truck, but before I turned the ignition on, I prayed, *"Dear Lord don't let any of this stuff fall off the truck."* I put the key in and turned it, and suddenly there was this loud voice (Sue cannot hear well, and she had a book on tape in the player). I looked at her and said, *"I did not expect him to answer so soon."*

Well, Sue cracked up. We laughed all the way to the landfill and didn't lose a thing. Thank you, Lord!
—Juli C.

Woman's Wisdom
"Whatever a man can do – I can fix!"
—*Anonymous*

Sue's Hambone

I bought me a ham and was going to put it in the crockpot on the back porch so as not to heat up the kitchen. I went out and tried to put it in, but it was too big. So, I took it back to the kitchen and cut off some, took it back to the porch, and it was still too big. I took it back again and cut some more off. I did this three times and now the bone was too long. On the way back to the kitchen, I tripped and dropped the ham! I had to go to the storage house and get a hacksaw to cut the bone. After all that, I was too mad to eat! —*Lottie G.*

Lottie G.

Red Hair

I was visiting South Carolina, and there were a lot of people at Mama's house. I sat down next to Mama on the swing. She looked over at me and said, "Jitterbug, your hair is red!"

I replied, "Ma it's a miracle, I turned forty and God blessed me with this beautiful red hair."

Ma said, "Smart mouth!" —*Juli C.*

Red Hair

"Givers should set limits. Takers will not!"
—*Anonymous*

Bike-in-Bag

When John David was little, he would come and spend the summer with his grandma and grandpa. This one time, he was packing for his trip. He was coming by train, and he was about eight years old. He asked his dad if he could bring his bike. John said no, you can only take what you can fit in your suitcase. When Ned picked him up at the train station in Denmark, he lifted his suitcase and said, "Boy, what's you got in here, rocks?" When Ned delivered him and John D. unzipped his suitcase, he had his bike all taken apart and in the suitcase with one set of underwear, one shirt, and a pair of summer shorts! —*Lottie G.*

Eats Like Horses

My friend and I were talking, and he said, "My two boys eat like horses."

I said, "Yeah, mine too."

Then he said, "When will they stop eating so much?"

I said, "When they start paying for the feed."

—*Johnny B.*

Swimming Lessons

I took GiAnna for her first swimming lesson; she spent the whole hour telling the instructor how to swim.
—*Jordan P.*

Bad Meat

Tommy and I bought a new freezer, and we had not had it long when it stopped working (it was full of meat). We called Best Buy where we bought it, and they said it was out of warranty! Tommy said, "Well I'm bringing it back and I'll need help getting it off the truck." He took it back with all that rotten meat! They unloaded it, and Tommy cut a trail. —*Winkey M.*

Good Advice

Mandy's boyfriend came all the way from Myrtle Beach to North Augusta to ask my permission to marry Mandy. I told him, "Yes, but I have one piece of advice for you. Do not let your in-laws interfere in your business." I looked over at my wife Reba, and she was giving me a dirty look! —*Robert B.*

"Never go to bed mad. Stay up and fight."
—*Phillis Diller*

The Mystery of the Bugaloo Hum

When I was a teenager, we lived in Covington, Louisiana. My best friend Ken Arnault lived across the street. His dad owned oil and gas wells, and he would let Ken and me go with him to inspect the wells. This one time we saw this big, low, metal dome and asked what it was. Mr. Arnault said it was a horn off a big cargo ship. We asked if we could have it, and he said yes.

Jerry, Ken, Tom, & John David

So, we loaded it on the truck and took it back to the Arnaults' house. One night Ken and I decided to test it. We attached an air hose to it, and it emitted this deep, low, loud hum that made the concrete garage floor vibrate. Late one night after everyone had gone to bed, we opened the garage door with the lights off and let it blast and quickly closed the door. We went outside and you could see lights come on all over the neighborhood. Boy was this fun! We waited a few weeks and did it again. We kept this up for months. It was not long before there was an article in the newspaper about the "Mysterious Bugaloo Hum." —*Ken C.*

A sign in my Dentist's Office "Control your kid, or we will give him an expresso and a puppy when you leave."

Snow In Florida

Ken, Jewell, and I were watching a movie; Leah was in her room playing. After a while we smelled something coming from her room. Ken got up to check, and Leah had squirted a large bottle of baby powder all over her room! It took hours to clean it up, and Ken was not happy! Later Leah slipped into my room, got in bed with me, and said, "Just think Aunt Pealey, I made it snow in Florida."—*Pealey H.*

Traffic Jam

My friend Margaret and I were in Knoxville, Tennessee. Margaret was driving down this hill and spotted a caravan of camels crossing the street (the circus was in town). She stopped the car, grabbed her camera, and jumped out, leaving the door open. She hollered for me to, "Come on!" Well, I got out and followed her. She got some great photos and after a while I said, "We had better go back." We started back up the hill and there standing next to the car was this BIG policeman with a line of traffic behind him. He was not smiling!
—*Olive M.*

Prepping for Surgery

Back in the seventies a friend of mine, who was a nurse, told me this story. She was prepping this man for surgery (back then they would shave most of the body) and he said, "You can take all of that brush between my legs, but leave that pine in the middle." —*Juli C.*

"Children are God's way of punishing you for having sex!" —*Ann Richards, Former Governor of Texas*

Gag Gifts

One year, the whole family had gathered for Thanksgiving. We could not all be together for Christmas, so we decided we would exchange gifts early that year (gag gifts). Joe got a limb with a knot on the end to use as a golf club. Brother Bobby gave me a paint-by-number set. Katie got a pair of high-top tennis shoes on platforms—someone had glued two-by-fours together and nailed them to the bottom of the shoes and painted them! —*Juli C.*

Altar Guild

Years ago, at St. Thaddeus Church, there was a misprint in the Sunday bulletin. It stated that the Altar Guild needed some "hookers." I called and asked about it and the priest told me I was too late. The job had already been filled. —*Mary P.*

Lent

I gave a talk for our Ladies Lunch Bunch (a group of ladies all over sixty years old). There were about twenty people there. Usually there are thirty or more. Mary said to me, "I guess everyone gave up fun for lent."

I replied, "Why couldn't they have given up sex?" Mary could not believe I said that! —*Juli C.*

Gambling

Regan (nine years old) and I were at the store, and he asked, "What's Lotto mean?" I told him that it was gambling, and I explained how it was done. Regan asked if I had ever done it before.

I said, "Yeah a few times, but I don't do it anymore because I always lost."

Regan then asked, "Papa, can we buy a ticket?" and I said, "Yeah we'll get one."

We did and took it out to the car. I let Regan scratch off the ticket and we had won $20, so we went back in the store and got our winnings. I told the lady to give us two tens. I gave Regan ten and I kept ten.

Regan asked, "Papa can we buy ten more tickets?"

I said, "Yeah, if you use your ten dollars." He did not like that idea. I told Regan, "Now boy, don't go home and tell your Mama about us gambling," knowing that was exactly what he would do.

He asked, "Why not?"

I said, "Well she won't like it."

He said, "But why not?"

I said, "Well, your other Papa is a preacher, and I don't want anyone to know that I let you gamble."

Then Regan said, "But what if I had won a million dollars?"

I told him, "If you had won a million dollars then everyone would love you and gambling wouldn't be a bad thing."

—*John B.*

"Don't offer me advice. Give me money."
—*Old Spanish Proverb*

New Hair

I was losing my hair and became concerned, so I went to the dermatologist. She told me that I had male pattern baldness and told me to buy Rogaine for women (a lotion with male hormones in it). Well, I did, and I started growing some fuzz on my head. As an extra bonus, I grew a nice, dark, thick beard! —*Juli C.*

We Love To Read

Mama loved to read as do most of her kids. One day she gave me a book and said, "It's a good book, but there is some bad language in it, so just skip over that part." —*Lottie G.*

A New Knee

They had Ralph sedated for surgery (he was having a knee replaced). He told them to make sure that they put the knee on right because he did not want one leg walking backwards. —*Pealey H.*

Barney Fife

There is a column in the newspaper where people call in and make comments; this is one I read. "Is Lindsey Graham, our State Senator, the illegitimate son of Barney Fife?" —*Juli C.*

Great Gas Mileage

Ethan had bought himself a new Lexus, and he kept bragging about the great gas mileage he got. His friends Bill and Rik started sneaking over at night and adding gas to his tank. The more they added, the more Ethan bragged. Then they started siphoning out gas and Ole Ethan started complaining about his gas mileage. He took it back to the dealership and had them check it out, but they could not find anything wrong. Poor Ethan was convinced that he had bought a lemon and tried to get the dealer to take it back. Bill and Rick finally confessed to what they had done! —*Juli C.*

Morning Coffee

Every morning, I would fix Billy his coffee and put a laxative in his. One morning I fixed myself a cup and him one, but by the time I got back to the bedroom I could not remember which was mine and which was his. Katie asked, "Well did you figure out who got what?" and I said, "I think I got Billy's." —*Lottie G.*

Super Glue

Glen was falling down drunk, and he fell in the kitchen, hit his head on the corner of the cabinet, and tore his ear in half. The lower half was just hanging on. Now, I was not going to take him to the emergency room. I know him well. He would get there and pitch a fit, and they would call the police and have him locked up. Then I would have to bail him out! So, I decided to repair that ear myself! First, I cleaned it, then put antibiotic cream on it, then I got Josh to help hold the ear and I super-glued it together. The next day Glen looked like he had been run over by a bulldozer. He was swollen and black and blue. But when that ear healed, it was only a hair off. —*Marty L.*

Good Medicine

Glen was sick with something like the flu, so I doctored him. I gave him some antibiotics the vet had given me for my dog "Sister." Well, when Glen found out that I had given him dog medicine, he had a fit! He will not take medicine from me anymore. I told him not to worry about it unless he started chasing cars.
—*Marty L.*

The Stalker

Marty and Glen were in Daytona, Florida, for the Daytona 500 race. Marty had left something in the hotel room and had gone back up to get it, leaving Glen in the lobby. While she was waiting for the elevator to go down, a man came up, stood too close to her, and made her feel uncomfortable. She decided she did not want to get on the elevator with him. She turned and went to find the stairs. As she went through the door, she saw he was right behind her. She turned, grabbed his arm, and slung him over the railing down *three flights of stairs!* She went back, got on the elevator, went to the lobby, and told the desk clerk that there was a man in the stairwell, and he may be hurt. Then she left the hotel. — *Ned B.*

After I heard this story, I asked Marty if it was true, and she said, "Yeah."

I then asked, "But Marty, what if you had killed him!"

Marty said, "Oh Lord I hope not. That's the only commandment I haven't broken!" —*Juli C.*

"Hearing a singer sing nothing but high notes is like hearing a steam whistle blow for five minutes." —*Juli C.*

Let It Go

Deana came to visit me, and she brought five-year-old GiGi with her. Twiddle, Ralph, Johnny, and Maria stopped by to visit and as they were leaving, we all walked out onto the front porch to say goodbye. Gi started singing, "Let it Go," the theme song from the movie *Frozen*. When she finished, Johnny pulled out a dollar and gave it to her. Well, Gi sang it again, this time a little louder. Ralph gave her a dollar, and she sang it again, even louder! She ended up with $5! Deana finally said, "Enough!" We all laughed so hard. That child was really belting it out. —*Juli C.*

Trashy People

Cousin Earl (a Baptist preacher) went calling on this trashy family. While Earl was talking to them, a rat ran up his pants leg. After he got the rat out, he cut his visit short. —*Lottie G.*

Handicap Parking

I dropped Winkey off at Walmart. She had to pick up only one thing, so I told her to call me on the cell phone when she was coming out. Meanwhile, I drove around but could not find a parking space, so I parked in the handicap parking (which I never do!). I had just parked and all of a sudden, I hear sirens and tires squealing as three police cars slid in all around me. I thought, *Dang, they're serious about this handicap parking.* I was waiting for them to drag me out, throw me on the ground, and cuff me. Then I saw a police officer chasing this black guy out of the store, and I said, "Thank you, Lord, it's not me they want." Winkey called and I told her where I was parked and not to be surprised at all the police cars that had me blocked in. Boy was I anxious to get out of there. *I swear I will never park in the handicap parking again!*
—*Tommy M.*

All Dressed-Up

One Easter, my girls and I dressed up alike—same dresses, same shoes, same hats—and went to church. Afterwards we all went to Ryan's for lunch. As we were leaving, this older couple was coming in. The man looked at his wife and said, "Well Margaret, looks like we missed the entertainment." —*Maria B.*

Outsmarted

While we were living in Louisiana, Hank Stram (head football coach for the New Orleans Saints) lived down the street from us. He always drove really fast down our street. One day the Arnoult boys and I heard him coming so we grabbed a hose with a high-pressure nozzle on it that was lying in the yard. Ole Hank had his windows open with his dog Rocky riding with him. As he came by, we squirted him upside the head! He came to a screeching halt, and we all hid behind a big bush. He saw my mom in the front yard and went and told on us. The next day we boys were playing in the front yard when Hank came by. He stopped, called us over to his "Big Ole Lincoln," and said, "Boys, let us call a truce. You can come down to my house any time. I have got a refrigerator in the garage that I keep full of sodas and snacks and y'all can just help yourselves. I only ask one thing. Do not hurt my dog." After that, we would ride our bikes down to Hank's and load up! —*Ken C.*

Bad Memory

Pealey said to Winkey, "My memory is getting bad."
 Winkey asked, "How bad is it?"
 Pealey said, "What are you talking about?"
 I stood there listening to them and just laughed.
—*Juli C.*

Half-a-Door

Jordan was working for Woodruff Construction. At the time they were doing sub-contract work for Home Depot, installing residential doors. Jordan was called to go to this house for a site visit to replace a door. Amy at Home Depot asked Jordan what he would charge for a service call and Jordan said "$30." When she sent over the work order, she was only paying him $14.95 for the job! Jordan called Amy and asked what half of the door she wanted installed. She said, "I don't know what you are talking about."

Jordan said, "You're only paying me half, so I'll install half a door."

Amy got huffy and said, "Do I need to get my supervisor involved?"

Jordan said, "Yeah, and while you have him on the phone, ask him which half he wants!"

The next day Kelley, the owner of the company, was called to go to the same location, and they paid him $50!
—*Grandma Juli*

The Plan

Aunt Helen was in a nursing home, and her son Tony went to visit her. He saw a puddle of water on the floor and said to his mom, "That's dangerous - someone could slip and get hurt."

Aunt Helen said, "Yeah, that's the plan." —*Robert B.*

The Power of B.O.

Me and Pa were out at Sunnybrook. We came up to these two brothers who lived in a shack near the creek. These men only bathed in the summertime in the creek. We spoke to them, and one said, "There is a wasp nest over there. We should get it and use the larva for fish bait."

The other brother said, "Who's gonna rob it?"

The first brother said, "I will." He did not have a shirt on and reached one hand under his arm, rubbed it good, then reached over to the nest and, may God strike me dead, the wasps all flew away!" —*The Babe*

The Arithmetic Dog

One day a dog came through the yard, and he was holding up his back leg. Daddy said, "That's an arithmetic dog. He's putting down three and carrying one." —*Robert B.*

Tongue Tied Granny

I was taking Braedon and Kaity to the pool to swim with their cousins Micah, Blake, and Leah. I said to Braedon, "Y'all go ahead and get in the water. I am going to sh—in the shade."
    Braedon looked at me and said, "Grandma!"
    I said, "Oh you know what I mean."
—*Grandma Pealey*

Fish Eyes

There were three things Mama loved: bread with her meals, fish, and liver pudding. One day Lottie, Winkey, Mama, and I were going to visit Pealey and Mickey in North Carolina. On the way, we stopped in Saluda and bought liver pudding. We decided to take some to Mickey, but when we got there, Mickey said he did not like liver pudding. Well, every time someone mentioned food, Mama would say, "Let's eat liver pudding." That night Mickey took us to a nice restaurant. Mama ordered flounder and when they brought it to the table it was a whole fish with its head on! Mama's eyes got big, and she reared back. From the look on her face, I could tell she was not happy! "I can't eat anything that's looking back at me," she said. She kept on fussing as she picked up her fork and started eating. When she finished there was nothing left but the head and bones. She had picked it clean. I am sure if it had not been for those eyes, she would have picked the head clean, too!
—*Twiddle J.*

Drunk On Liver Pudding

A bunch of us went to Saluda; we stopped at this meat packing plant and bought liver pudding. We also stopped and bought some saltine crackers. We sat in Hardee's parking lot and ate. Mama ate so much it ran her blood pressure up, and she was acting drunk.
—*Lottie G.*

Flushing the Toilet

Mama and Daddy came up from Florida to visit. I was living in their old house, and it did not have a bathroom. We had a toilet in the back yard. Billy saw Ned (four or five years old) coming out of the toilet and asked him, "Boy did you flush the toilet?" Ned said, "I tried, but I couldn't find the flusher." —*Lottie G.*

Third Grade

I had gone to Charlotte to babysit my grandchildren. Chris was taking Michelle away for a few days. Kaity asked me to help her with her math homework. I tried and Kaity finally said, "Grandma, how long has it been since you were in the third grade?" —*Grandma Pealey*

Homework

Sam came home from school one day and said, "Grandma, I don't want to hurt your feelings, but don't help me with my homework anymore!"
—*Grandma Marty*

Bandits

While visiting Jackson Hole, Wyoming, Deana and I were taking a rafting trip down the Snake River, and our boatman told this story about this man who owned a hunting lodge on the river. This man's business was taking people out big game hunting. He had this man from back east call and say that he was bringing some friends with him, and he wanted them to have an exciting time. The guide told him where to meet him up the river. The guide then got some friends to dress like bandits with guns. They bushed-wacked the visitors, roughed them up, tied them up, robbed them, put them in the boat, took them down the river to the lodge, took them out of the boat, untied them and asked, "Was that exciting enough for you?" —*Juli C.*

Diet Coke

When my Grandson Jason was little, we were at a fast-food restaurant, and Jason said, "I don't want no damn Diet Coke." I am sure he heard this from his dad.
—*Granny Lottie*

Fleas

We were talking about fleas, and Marty said, "Yeah, fleas will jump off a dog to get on me!" —*Juli C.*

Tom Did It

One day Billy was fussing at Jason about something he had done. Jason (three years old) said, "Tom did it. I was standing on the clothesline and saw him do it." Tom was the cat. —*Granny Lottie*

Pear Lips

I am sure you have seen people with a "hare lip." Well, Winkey had "Pear Lips." She came to the house for something and while she was there, she decided she would pick some pears from the tree in the backyard to take home. She reached up to pull off a pear and one fell from high up in the tree and hit her in the mouth! It busted both upper and lower lip! She started mumbling, "Oh man, I'm gonna have sores on both lips!" Her lips were starting to swell, so I gave her ice to put on them. I should have super-glued the cuts on her lips. It took a month for them to heal. —*Juli C.*

Birth Control

I had a telemarketer call and asked if my husband and I were having any trouble with birth control. I said, "No. I'm seventy-four and Billy is seventy-eight!" —*Lottie G.*

"A whistling woman and a crowing hen never came to no good end." —*John Leopard*

Fighting in Rose's

Carl (a dwarf) was shopping with his son Rusty at Rose's. Rusty hid under a rack of clothes and when Carl finally found him, he went under the rack and started spanking Rusty. The manager saw them and said, "You boy's stop that fighting." —*Twiddle J.*

Antique Rugs

We sisters were in Savannah, Georgia. As we were walking past an antique shop, there was a truck parked at the curb, and a man was unloading antique rugs and had them laid out on the sidewalk.

I said to Sue, "I guess we'll have to walk around those rugs."

The man heard me and said, "Camels have peed on these rugs for hundreds of years, so it's okay for you to walk on them." And we did! —*Juli C.*

The Hysterectomy

Frances was scheduled to have a hysterectomy. She was telling her cousin Larry about it, and he said, "You know after you have that done, you can't have any more children."

Frances said, "I'm seventy-one years old!" —*Juli C.*

Speeding Ticket

Back in the late seventies, I was doing a Renaissance Festival in New Orleans. Joe wanted to go with me, so I told him he would have to dress in a period costume. He agreed and I dressed him in burgundy tights, tan leather slippers with the toes turned up, a print tunic with gold trim that matched the tights, a blouse with full sleeves, and a wig. We were running late, so Joe was speeding on the causeway (a twenty-four-mile-long bridge over Lake Pontchartrain) when the police pulled up beside us and stopped. The bridge is two lanes in each direction, so all traffic came to a stop. He made Joe stand outside the car while he gave him a ticket. Of course, Joe blamed me and was mad the rest of the day!
—*Juli C.*

Hiding Gifts

When Ken was four years old, he found his birthday presents that I had hidden under the bed.

I scolded him and asked, "What were you doing under the bed?"

He replied, "Why didn't you hide them in the attic where you put all the Christmas gifts?" —*Juli C.*

"A bargain is something you can't use at a price you can't resist." —*Old Saying*

"I would agree with you, but then we would both be wrong!" —*Anonymous*

The Check-Up

Ralph was retiring in a few weeks and told Twiddle to start looking for health insurance. She called Pealey and asked her what insurance company she used. Pealey gave her the information and told Twiddle she would have to have a check-up. Well, Twiddle had not been to a doctor in twenty-four years! So, she goes for a check-up. Fast forward a few days. Sue, Pealey, Winkey, and I went to Twiddle's to pick her up because we were meeting Katie for lunch. While at Twiddle's, she starts telling us about her check-up. She said the doctor was giving her a pap test and said that from where he was sitting, the back of her eyes looked really good!

Well, Pealey pops up and said, "You know, you didn't have to get a check-up to get insurance."

Twiddle's mouth dropped open. She jumped up and started dancing around and hollerin', "I am mad, really mad, boy are you going to get it! I cannot believe you did this to me; I am so mad!"

Pealey said, "It was only a joke- I'm getting even with you for setting the floor on fire when we were kids and blaming it on me!"

The Brickettes

Twiddle said, "Well, now you have a snake by the tail and it's going to bite. You just don't know when or where."

Pealey said, "Just go ahead and punish me and get it over with." While in the car, the six of us sisters were talking about pierced ears. Pealey started to say that she needed to have hers redone but caught herself in mid-sentence.

Twiddle jumped in and said, "Oh, I'll do it for you. I have a new hole punch and I'll start at the top and work my way to the bottom!"

Pealey said, "Do not be mean to me. I am still in mourning." We all laughed so hard our stomachs hurt.

At lunch, Pealey said the blessing. First, she prayed for Kyle, then for the food, and last she said, "And Lord, don't let Twiddle hurt me!"

What a fun day! —*Juli C.*

Hush Puppies

Rik and I were visiting South Carolina, and we took Mama out to Red Lobster for dinner. She ordered fish, and when they brought her food she said, "Where are the hush puppies?" I explained that they did not serve hush puppies and that they only had cheddar biscuits.

"Well," said Mama, "you would think that a seafood restaurant would have hush puppies." She fussed all during dinner and all the way home.

Later, Rik said to me, "The next time we take your Mama to eat fish, we'll stop at Captain D's and buy hush puppies to take with us!" —*Juli C.*

"Put all your eggs in one basket, and then watch that basket." —*Mark Twain*

Gator Hunting

Keith and I went alligator hunting on the Savannah River. We found a gator and shot arrows with line on them but kept missing him. At last, I threw a gaffing hook and snagged the gator. That gator started going into the bushes on the side of the river. Keith was working the motor, and I told him to back up. He tried, but the motor was tangled up in line. Then that gator started rolling, and the line got twisted up around him. Now that gator had his back legs in the boat, his head under the water, and he was slapping me upside the head with his tail, but I held on! Then Keith hollered, "Stop! Stop! You are gonna hurt him!"—*John David B.*

Preachers

Mama was in the hospital and there was a gang of people in her room visiting. Huck said, "I bet if you threw a cat in that room, you would hit three preachers before it touched the floor." —*Robert B.*

Winkey Cannot Tell a Joke

Ned said to Winkey, "Tell that joke I told you last week." Winkey started to tell it and instead of saying "harelip, harelip" for the punch line, she said, "peg leg, peg leg," which made no sense at all. Now every time Winkey starts to tell a joke, Robert will say, "Peg leg, peg leg," and everyone cracks up! —*Juli C.*

Marty & Winkey

"I hope that life is not a big joke, because I do not get it." —*Jack Handey*

Wrong Car

My sister Marsha and I went to rent some videos. It was raining really hard, so Marsha stayed in the car. I went in and got the movies, came out, and got into a car that looked just like mine. I put the movies down, looked over, and I saw Marsha in the car next to me, waving. I then realized I had gotten in the wrong car! I quickly got out and ran and got in my car and drove home. Then Marsha asked, "Where are the movies?" I went out to my car and looked, and the movies were not there. I had left them in that other car! I ended up having to pay $70 for those movies. Robert sure got mad. —*Reba B.*

Fighting in the Parking Lot

Kelley and I were in my car, and Kelley was driving. We stopped, and I got out and went into a store, leaving Kelley in the car. Some man got in the passenger's seat, looked over at Kelley, and put up his fists wanting to fight. The man's wife was in the car next to them, watching and laughing her head off! —*Deana W.*

Hijacker

I had been shopping and came out and got into what I thought was my SUV. I looked over and there sat this big black man. He said, "I think that's your car over there." At first, I thought he was hijacking me!
—*Pealey H.*

Tree Frogs

Chris bought a house and there was a pond on the property behind him. There were tree frogs everywhere. Every time he looked out the windows all he would see were frogs all over the glass! He called the exterminator to get rid of them and they said, "We don't do frogs!"
—*Pealey H.*

Canning

Back in the 1940s, Daddy built Mama this canning setup in the back yard; she could can twice as much this way. One day, she was canning beans and a neighbor called the police and told them Mama was making moonshine!
—*Lottie G*

"Make somebody happy today. Mind your own business!" —*Ann Landers*

Driving to Work

Back in the 1940s, Daddy worked in the cotton mill. Most days he would walk to work because we lived only a few blocks away. One day he drove the car, and after work he walked home and did not see his car! He thought someone had stolen it. He started following the tire tracks (the streets were dirty back then). They led him back to the mill where he had left the car!
—*Lottie G.*

The Sermon

At church this morning, the preacher was giving his sermon and said, "The grass may look greener on the other side of the fence; in fact, it probably is because it's growing on a cesspool!" —*Pealey H.*

Peanuts

Cousin Earl told this while preaching this morning. This preacher went to the hospital to visit a lady. There was a cup of peanuts on the table and the preacher started eating some. When he got ready to go, he apologized for eating all her peanuts. The lady said, "That is okay. I had already licked the chocolate off them!" —*Lottie G.*

Going to the Outhouse

Late one night I was going to the outhouse. As I passed under the pear tree, a cat jumped out of the tree onto my head. It scared me so bad that there was not much need to go on to the toilet after that! —*Lottie G.*

Stampeding Cows

In 1958, Daddy moved the family to Cairo, Georgia. We stayed there for a month before going to Pahokee, Florida. This was in August, and I can tell you it gets mighty hot in South Georgia that time of year. The old farmhouse that we stayed in was close to a river, and it was swampy and humid. We kids were bored so we decided to have some fun. There was this pecan orchard next to the house that was fenced in, and there were cows in there. First, we took a large empty can, punched a hole in the center of the bottom with a nail, and then poked a string of woven cord through the Hole. We tied a knot so the cord would not come out,

L-R Walter, Johnny, Carl, Pealey, & Winkey

then got some rosin from a pine tree and rubbed it on the cord. When you pulled on the cord, it made an awful sound (Daddy had shown us how to do this). To test our cans, we went up the road a way where there were some black men working in the field. We hid on the edge of the woods and started pulling on our strings. Those men stopped and listened. We did it again and they threw down their hoe's and ran! We laughed and laughed. Boy, was this fun! Next, we went over to the pecan pasture. Walter, Johnny, and I got inside the fence to stampede the cows, and we made the other kids stay outside the fence. The cows did not pay any attention to us until we started to pull on our strings making this weird noise. Well, they cut a trail! We were belly laughing so hard…that is until we saw this big black bull coming at us full speed! Well, Walter and I ran for the fence and got over just in time, but Johnny was too far from the fence, so he ran to the nearest tree and climbed it. That bull snorted and butted that tree, but Johnny held on! After about an hour, the bull got tired and left. Johnny finally came home. That was the last time we stampeded cows! —*Juli C.*

Digging to China

When we lived in the White House, Sue, Walter, Johnny, and I decided to dig a tunnel to China. We had heard in school that China was on the other side of the world so we figured that it would be closer to go through the earth than around it. We chose a spot behind the smoke house and started digging. We went in for dinner (lunch), and Mama asked what we were doing, and we said, "Just playing." Well, we dug all day. I guess we got down about eight or nine feet (this was sandy dirt).

Easter Picnic, 1974
Walter, Jerry, Ken, Joni, Vicki, Leigh, & Connie

We took turns getting in the hole digging and hauling out the dirt and by the end of the day we were dirty and exhausted, but proud of what we had accomplished. When Daddy came home and saw that hole, he got mad and told us to fill it back up! The next day after we filled that hole, we had a meeting and decided to build an Indian village and play cowboys and Indians. Besides, it would take at least three days to dig to China!
—*Juli C.*

Fighting In the Basement

Back when Lottie and my kids were small, we had planned to take them to Greggs Park for a picnic. Well, Stevie and Bubba had been fighting all morning, and when Lottie told them to get in the car, they said they did not want to go. So, Lottie got mad and drug them both to the basement and locked them in. Now it was summertime. There was no floor in the basement, just dirt. At some point in the afternoon, Tony Leopard came by and heard them fighting.

He asked, "What are you boys doing in there?"

They hollered, "Let us out! Mama locked us in here."

Tony said, "If your Mama put you in there, I ain't letting you out," and went on down the hill.

When Lottie and I got back, she let the boys out. They sure were glad to see us. They had spent the afternoon fighting in that black dirt, and all you could see were the white of their eyes. —*Juli C.*

Mule Funeral

One day Walter, Jewell, Johnny, Doll, and I went way back into the woods to play. We found an old dead mule and decided to give it a funeral. We sang some songs for a while, then we prayed, preached, and shouted. Then we sang some more. This went on all morning. We did this every day for about a week until the blowflies and buzzards got so bad, we could not get near that mule. I guess that old mule went to Heaven. If he did not, it was not because he did not get a good funeral! —*Lottie G.*

L-R Lottie Doll, Jewell, Ella Mae

Planting the Indian Way

One time Daddy decided to plant his corn the Indian way. He went fishing and cut up the fish and put a piece in each hole with the seed corn. After a few days, those fish got to stinking. Something came along at night, dug up the fish, and ate them. —*Juli C.*

Tongue Tied

"I'll teach you to hit me in the door with that dad burn face." —*John Leopard*

The Perfect Hiding Place

Grandpa Leopard sold moonshine during the depression. The law would come raid him. Well, usually someone would warn him about the raid. He would take his moonshine into the pasture and dig holes with a post-hole digger. A ½ gallon jug would fit perfect in the hole. Then he would cover the holes with cow patties. The Fed's would walk all over the pasture and could not find his moonshine. They would say they knew he was selling it, but they could not find it. Grandpa was a smart fellow." Ain't nobody gonna mess with cow patties." —*Lottie G.*

Racing Cars

Back in 1957, Bub and Gene each had a 1955 car. One had a Chevy, and the other had a Ford (I do not remember who had what). I remember they were always arguing about which was fastest. I happened to be at Grandma's one day when they decided to go race and prove once and for all which was fastest. They took me along as their witness! They decided to use the new four-lane highway. It was paved but not open yet. Bub put me in his car, and we started off neck and neck. I remember looking at the speedometer, and the needle was past 125 mph! About that time, the hood flew up! But Bub would not stop! He put his head out the window to see where he was going. Gene won the race, but Bub would not admit defeat because he was driving under a handicap! —*Juli C.*

The Drunk

Uncle Lee came home drunk one night. Aunt Ellen said, "Drunk again," and Uncle Lee said, "Yeah, me too."
—*Told to Lottie by Uncle Euman*

"Uncle Lee was a skinny little man, and Aunt Ellen was a decent size woman." —*Lottie G.*

Water Business

We would put water in a jug and go up to the pine thicket where Midland Valley High School is today. There were always a bunch of men playing cards. Our Granddaddy was our best customer. Water payment came out of the next pot. —*Johnny B.*

Ban on BB Guns

Back in 1958, Johnny was fifteen years old. He and Walter had walked the two miles to town to go to the movies. When they got to the theater, Walter met this cute girl and told Johnny to get lost. Well, Johnny got mad (and it did not take a lot to make him mad). He started walking home and realized he had his slingshot in his pocket. There were streetlights on every corner for two miles, and he did not miss a one! Two days later, on the front page of the newspaper was a big heading, "BAN ON BB GUNS." —*Juli C.*

The Siren

One summer, Joe and I had gone to New York to visit his family. His mom lived close to a firehouse, and every day at noon they would blow the siren. Ken loved that sound (he was about four years old). He practiced making that sound and got really good at it. On the way home we stopped at Myrtle Beach for a few days. Back then the road between Myrtle Beach and Aiken was a two-lane road. Well, Joe could not stand for another car to get in front of him, and he spent a couple of hours passing all those other cars. Finally, he was in the lead. No one in front of him. That is when Ken decided to practice his siren sound! Joe whipped the car off to the side of the road, thinking the police were after him. We sat there while all those cars he had passed went zooming by! I wanted to laugh, but Joe was so mad I did not dare. —*Juli C.*

Twiddle's Kitchen

When Twiddle and Ralph were building their house in Sweetwater, Twiddle told Ralph that she did not want a kitchen. (Twiddle does not like to cook.)

Ralph said, "We have to have a kitchen if we ever want to sell the house."

Twiddle said, "If I have to have a kitchen, all I want in it is a microwave and a vending machine!" —*Juli C.*

It is Good to Know the Ten Commandments

This is a story about Kyle, Katie and Marc's son. It happened at our annual picnic before Easter. Joni and Vicki hid the eggs, then gathered all the kids. They soon learned that was not quite right because the older kids found all the eggs before the little ones did. So, to be fair, they decided to hide the eggs again, allowing the younger ones to hunt for a while before calling the others. When they called for Kyle's age group, the children took off running. Everyone wanted to get there first. I began walking towards the woods to watch the excitement. Kyle was trailing along beside me.

I looked down and said, "Kyle, you better run before they find all the eggs."

He replied, "I've been running like hell—oops!" I supposed he realized what he had said and to whom he had said it. So like lighting, he took off!

When it was time to eat, I fixed my plate and noticed that Kyle was beside me again with his plate. I sat at the table, and Kyle asked if he could sit next to me.

I said, "Yes." He sat down and looked at me and said, "Aunt Pealey, I've been learning the Ten Commandments, you want to hear 'em?"—*Pealey H.*

Sheba

While living in Louisiana, one nice day, I was sitting in the swing on the upper verandah and reading. My dog Sheba was below and sleeping in the shade of some bushes. A garbage truck came down the street and stopped. This black man got out, and when he got halfway down the driveway, Sheba came out barking. The man turned and ran and jumped on the hood of the truck! After I got control of my laughing, I went down and rescued him. Sheba weighed all of twelve pounds, but that man was not taking any chances. —*Juli C.*

"If it can lick, it can bite!" —*Old Saying*

New Job

Jordan's first day as operation manager, he avoided two lawsuits, hired one person, fired one person, and kept one employee from quitting. Whew! —*Deana W.*

Easter Picnic

We were having our Easter picnic at Bobby's house, and I was sitting on one side of a picnic table. Earl and Pat came and sat down across from me, then Rik sat next to them. When I finished eating, I got up, and all three of them hit the ground! —*Juli C.*

Blue Carpet

Back in the early seventies, Lottie and Billy bought a new car—a blue Chevy. Lottie went shopping and put a gallon jug of bleach on the floor in the back. Well, the lid was not on tight, and it spilled all over that blue carpet! When she got home and opened the door, all that pretty blue carpet was bleached white! Well, she knew that Billy would pitch a fit when he saw it. Now Lottie was no dim wit. Back to the store she went and bought some blue dye. She dyed that carpet, and Billy never knew what had happened. —*Juli C.*

Mooned Over Lake Pontchartrain

Daddy, Mama, Lottie, Robert, and Reba came to visit me in Louisiana; I had planned to take them into New Orleans to the French Quarter. Daddy did not want to go, so the rest of us went. Coming home that night, I was driving on the Causeway when this car pulled up next to me. I looked over and saw that we were being mooned! Then the car sped on. I said, "Did y'all see that!" Everyone except Mama said, "Yeah," and laughed. Mama insisted she did not see anything. Well, I drove fast and passed the car, got in front of it, and slowed down. They knew what I wanted. They passed and mooned us again! Mama still said she did not see a thing. We all laughed the rest of the way home. —*Juli C.*

Ruts in the Road

One day Daddy, my friend Ed, and I were in Daddy's old truck going down this old dirt road.

Pa said, "These ruts are so bad a plane couldn't fly over them."

Later, Ed asked Pa if he had ever plowed a mule. Pa said, "Yep, I spent more than twenty years using a mule's a-- for a compass! —*Ned B.*

Hootie

When Joe was little, he said something highly intelligent, and I said, "You're smarter than a tree full of owls." That is how he got the nickname "Hootie." —*Robert B.*

Joe B.

Fighting in the Dark

One of my growing up memories was when Carl, Robert, Donnie, Ronnie, Marty, and I would fight when Mama and Daddy would go off. We would get into Mama and Daddy's bedroom, turn the lights off, and meet in the middle of the room and fight. Well, I was always a chicken and would hide under the bed. It did not take long before they found me out. They drug me out, and you know the rest! —*Katie W.*

Underwear or Panties?

One day I had a doctor's appointment and asked Brother Carl to keep Kyle and Mollie. While I was gone, Mollie had to use the bathroom. Well, Carl, not having girls, did not know how to help her. Mollie told him she could go by herself. She had been in the bathroom for about ten minutes when Carl went to the door and asked if she needed any help with her underwear. She let him know right away that she did not wear underwear. She wore panties! She was highly insulted! How was Carl to know? They only wear underwear at his house!
—*Katie W.*

First Snow

We do not get snow here in South Carolina very often. One winter night it snowed. The next morning when Robert looked out the window, he said, "Mama, them chickens have messed all over the yard!" —*Juli C.*

A Good Find

We were going to Salerno to camp for a week. Maria was pulling the boat. Johnny, Daddy, and I came along a little later. On the way, we saw a boat paddle and stopped and picked it up. A little later we saw a life jacket and stopped and picked it up. Then we saw a cooler. When Johnny picked up the cooler, it had his name on it! He had been picking up his own stuff. Maria had been slinging out all his stuff from the boat!
—*Carl B.*

Fighting Behind the Smokehouse

One day Carl and Ned were fighting behind the smokehouse. I was concerned that Ned would hurt Carl, so I went to help him out. I pulled Ned off Carl. Ned and I started fighting, and Carl got the pitchfork and started jabbing both of us! Carl said, "I can fight my own battles." And he did! —*Robert B.*

Hiding in the Closet

Once I was plundering in the closet. I heard Boney Grandma coming, so I hunkered down in the corner so she could not see me.

She opened the door and said, "Boy, what's you doing in there?"

I said, "Nothing," and Grandma said, "Well take nothing and get out."

As I came out, she grabbed me in a headlock and scrubbed the top of my head with her boney knuckles.
—Ned B.

Reality or Make-Believe?

If we got in the truck with Daddy and asked, "Where we were going?" he would always say, "Pocataligo." Last year, on my way to Hilton Head, I took a wrong turn and ended up on this unfamiliar road. I passed a sign that pointed to Pocataligo! I always thought he made that up. —*Robert B.*

Drinking Blood

When Jordan was little, Deana would sit in the back of the church with him so she could take him out if he started being bad. One day when he was about three or four years old, she decided to sit down front in the second pew. Jordan was being good and listening to what was being said. Then the priest started Holy Communion and said, "Drink this all of you, this is the blood of our Lord Jesus Christ." Jordan turned to his mom and in a loud voice said, "GROSS MOM, THEY'RE DRINKING BLOOD!" Well, the Priest and congregation cracked up! It took a while to get everyone calmed down and continue communion. —*Grandma Juli*

Jordan

Dinner At the Busbee House

I had stopped by the Busbees to visit with Mr. Busbee. We sat in the living room and talked about hunting. At noon sharp Mrs. Busbee called out, "Dinner's ready."

Mr. Busbee said, "Boy, come on and have dinner with us," so I did. There was a table full of food, with a big platter of fried chicken in front of me. Mr. Busbee said grace, and when I opened my eyes all that was left on that platter was a chicken back! The next time I was invited to eat there, I kept one eye open with a fork in my hand, and when the blessing was over, I had me a chicken leg. —*Tony N.*

Sneaking Candy

When I was a boy, Cousin Walter and I were playing. My pa came along (he had been to the store) and sat his bag of groceries on the porch and went into the house. Walter and I looked in the sack and saw what we thought was chocolate candy. We took it and ate the whole thing! We soon found out that it was not candy but Ex-Lax! —*Earl C.*

The Tea Jug

One year, all the boys got BB guns for Christmas. They were given instructions on what not to do. No shooting at cars, people, windows, dogs, or cats. Mama and us girls were cooking dinner. I had just finished making a gallon jug of tea (with two cups of sugar) when Huck walked into the kitchen, raised his gun, took aim, and POW! Shot that jug of tea. The jug shattered and tea went everywhere! Well, Huck got a beating and his gun taken away, and guess who got to clean that mess up!
—*Lottie G.*

"I'm not bossy. I just know what you should be doing!" —*Anonymous*

June Bugs

When we were little, Daddy and Uncle Euman would catch June bugs (big green iridescent bugs), tie a string around each bug's leg, and give us each one. The bug would fly, and we would run around the yard with our bugs. This was as much fun as flying a kite. —*Juli C.*

Dish Rag Soup

Cousin Tony was spending the night at our house. As he and Ned came through the kitchen, he grabbed a spoon and tasted what was in the pot on the stove. He gagged and said, "That's nasty." Turns out Mama was boiling her dish rags to get them clean. Ned said, "I think it needs a little salt!" —*Lottie G.*

The Briar Patch

When I was little, there was a big gully behind our house, and it was full of briars. Walter and Johnny had tied a rope on this limb that went out over the gully. We would all take turns swinging. Well, one day the limb broke, and guess who went flying into the briar patch. Jewell! —- *Winkey M.*

All My Cousins

When Micah was little, he was shy. When I would take him to family functions, I would tell him, "See all those kids? They're all your cousins." One day we were at the park and Micah saw a group of black children and asked, "Are all those my cousins?" —*Granny Winkey*

Jelly Bread

When Ken was little, I taught him to say the blessing. He would say, "God is great, God is good, let us thank him for our food. Bow our heads and let us pray, give us Lord our jelly bread!" When he went to his grandma's house, he always got a jelly bread. —*Juli C.*

New Bride

I brought my new bride home to visit. The next day I asked Pa what he thought of her. He said, "Well, the first one was a flat tire, but this one looks like she's all pumped up and ready to go!" —*Ronnie B.*

Boy's Come a-Courting

When Pealey and Winkey were teenagers, there were some boys at school who really liked them and decided to come to visit. Pa was sitting on the front porch and let them get as far as the front gate.

Then he said, "You boys have any business here?"

They said, "No sir."

Pa said, "Then good day to you!"

Those boys nearly fell all over each other trying to get away. —*Robert B.*

Hair Ball

One morning I was at Walmart having some fabric cut. The woman doing the cutting was mumbling and I asked what she had said. She said, "There was a man here, and he kept gagging and coughing. He sounded like he was trying to get up a hair ball!" We both laughed and laughed. That is the most fun I have ever had at Walmart. —*Juli C.*

Adding and Subtracting

For a while Steve would walk with me up at the school track. To keep track of how many laps we had walked, when we finished one, we would make a mark in the dirt. There were two men there walking and they saw us making marks, so they started marking their laps. The next time around, Steve added a few marks to theirs, next time he subtracted some. I do not know if those men ever figured out how many laps they made.
—*Lottie G.*

Sweeping Trash

One day Boney Grandma was sweeping the house. She swept up some bullets with the trash and put them in the heater in the living room! —*Robert B.*

Three Hairs

One time this old dog took up at our house. He had the mange so bad, all he had on his body was three hairs! So that is what I named him. Well, I doctored him with sulfur and burnt motor oil and soon he started growing hair. Larry G. said to me, "If your remedy works on Three Hairs, why don't you use it on Uncle Euman's bald head?" —*Lottie G.*

Saving a Frog's Life

Pealey and I were at the pool early one morning to do our water aerobics. I got in and saw a frog in the water. Knowing that he could not get out and would get caught in the drain and die, I took off one of my water shoes and tried to scoop him out. Well, he started swimming fast into the deep part of the pool, so I followed him and kept trying to flip him out. Suddenly, he turned and hopped on my chest! I started screaming, trying to get him off, and nearly drowned! Well, Pealey was watching and laughing her head off! I did not think that was so funny. —*Winkey M.*

Getting Even

Pa and Tony went hunting. When they got close to their deer stand, they saw where some guy had put up some yellow tape (the kind that the police use to tape off a crime scene). This man had put it up so he could find his deer stand early in the morning while it was still dark. Tony decided it would be fun to move the tape so the man would end up in the creek! The next time Pa and Tony went hunting, they found that that fellow did not take kindly to having his tape moved. He had cut the legs off of Pa's deer stand ladder. —*Carl B.*

Keeping Thieves Out

Rick came into the kitchen and said, "Well, I put a lock on the crawl space door."

I asked "Why? There is nothing under there."

He said, "To keep thieves from getting under the house, cutting a hole in the floor, coming in, and stealing our stuff."

"Oh, really," I said. "Why would anyone go to that much trouble when they can just come in the back door that you leave unlocked every night!" —*Juli C.*

Pa Wisdom

One day we were all sitting on the front porch after having a big dinner. I don't remember how the conversation got started, but I said, "I have always wanted a house with a big oak tree with a limb so I could have a swing on it." (I do love to swing)

Pa said, "Jitterbug, if that's what you want, you need to stop building your houses in pine thickets." —*Juli C.*

Ma's Girdle

Back when my boys were small, Mama and Daddy had moved back to Jordantown from Florida. Mama had wanted a girdle to hold her stomach in, so I bought her one. Well, she wanted me to take her shopping to buy school clothes for the kids. There were at least five of hers and my three. We headed for Augusta, and Mama was wearing her new girdle. The whole time we were shopping her girdle kept slipping down. She would struggle to pull it up, and it would slip down again. The more it slid, the more aggravated she got. We found clothes for all the kids except Carl. She could not find anything to fit him. By the time we left the store, her face was as red as a beet, and she was as mad as a wet setting hen! Mama never wore that girdle again.
—*Lottie G.*

Wringer Washer

Walter and James C. went rabbit hunting one day and killed some rabbits. James got blood on his jacket, and Walter asked me to wash it. I had an old wringer type washer in the basement. I put the jacket in, turned it on (it did not have an automatic off on it), and I went back upstairs and forgot all about it. That jacket washed all day long! When I finally thought about it and took it out, it was frayed and coming apart! But it sure was clean! James said he did not ever want me to wash anything for him again. —*Lottie G.*

Honey

I dreamed of Jewell coming to my house and knocking on the door in the middle of the night. Billy and I were falling all over each other trying to open the door. Jewell came in and she was terribly upset.

I asked what was wrong and she said, "Honey died."

I asked, "Who's Honey?" and she said, "I cannot talk about it. I will cry."

That is when I woke up, and I still do not know who Honey is. —*Lottie G.*

Sign on a safe at church "Don't touch. God is watching!"

Mama Loved Chitlings

Mama loved chitlings. She did not cook them often, and that was a good thing. One time she decided to cook them, and it had rained all day. Pa spent the entire day sitting in the smoke house, but Mama would not let us kids leave the house. God, what an awful smell! Another time she cooked them while we were at school, and when we got home, Jewell and I had to wash the dirty pots and pans she had left. Well, Jewell got mad and went outside and threw the frying pan in the trash barrel! Mama made her get it and clean it. —*Lottie G.*

"One day Mama cooked chitlings. Pa left home, and all of us kids spent the day in the woods, but no matter how far we went, we could not get away from that smell!" —*Juli C.*

Lonnie's Possum

One day Uncle Lonnie came to visit. This was before 1950, and he had a possum that he had killed and cleaned and wanted Mama to cook it for him. Mama did not like the idea, but Lonnie talked her into it. She swore she would never cook another possum because it smelled bad. I, however, did not think it smelled half as bad as the chitlings she loved! —*Juli C.*

"It is what it is, so deal with it!" —*Ken C.*

Damn Ole Japs

One Sunday morning back in the 1980s, Uncle Euman was at my house to eat dinner. I was cooking, and he was sitting in the living room reading the newspaper. He stopped to clean his glasses and noticed that they were made in Japan. He said, "Damn ole Japs, if I hadn't paid so much for these glasses, I would throw them down and stomp on them!" Uncle Euman had fought in WWII and hated Japs! —*Lottie G.*

Bad Boys

Back in the seventies, there were woods behind our house with a path that our newspaper boy used. Stevie and Bubba dug a hole in the path and put sticks and leaves over the hole. When Phillip came down the path on his bicycle, he hit that hole, and he and the newspapers went flying! Those boys would do that every few days. Finally, Phillip told me if I did not make them quit, he was not going to bring me the paper anymore. —*Lottie G.*

French Names

When I worked for a cell phone company, a woman called into customer service, and the dispatcher asked for her location. She said, "Pig`ion For`gay."

He asked, "Say that again?"

She repeated, "Pig`ion For`gay."

He finally figured out that she was saying was "Pigeon Forge" with a French accent. —*Deana W.*

Outlaw Chicken Soup

I was talking on the phone to Twiddle and telling her about all the different meals that I had made using rotisserie chicken. She said, "There has got to be a law against getting so many meals from one chicken!" So, I named one of the meals "Outlaw Chicken Soup."
—*Juli C.*

Christmas

I was reminiscing with Erin and Twiddle about when we were kids at Christmas. We were poor, and whatever we got at Christmas we had to share. Twiddle, Pealey, and I shared baby dolls, tea sets, etc. It was always exciting when a big package arrived from older sister Jewell because each gift was wrapped with our names on them (at home the gifts were put under the tree unwrapped). The best part was your gift belonged to you, and you did not have to share. Some years those were the only gifts we got. You never know how your actions will affect others. —*Winkey M.*

Strawberries

One day this farmer hauling a load of manure broke down in front of this mental hospital. Some of the patients walked over and asked what he was hauling, and the farmer said, "Manure."
    One patient asked, "What do you use it for?"
    The farmer said, "I put it on my strawberries."
    The patient said, "Call me crazy, but where I come from, we put whip cream on our strawberries."
—*Nora B.*

Snuff Can Bomb

When I was a kid, I was over at Grandma's house. Ned asked me to help him – he took an empty snuff can, filled it with gun powder from a shotgun shell, then we put a fuse in the lid, put the lid on the can, and took it down and placed it in the toilet. Ned lit the fuse, and we ran like turkeys. When it blew it lifted that toilet about ten inches off the foundation! —*David G.*

A Knowing

At 6:30 AM one morning, my neighbor was at my door, carrying her eighteen-month-old daughter, and crying. I asked what was wrong and she said, "I'm pregnant."
    I asked, "Are you sure?" and she said, "Yes."
    I asked, "How far along are you?"
    She said, "Since last night!"
    Sure enough, nine months later Phillip was born.
—*Carole W.*

Mama Having Another Baby

I had this dream; Mama was ninety-four years old, and she had just had another baby! And she was trying to give it to me, and I did not want it! Whew. That was not a dream. It was a nightmare! —*Lottie G.*

The Ark

A group of us were having breakfast at Hardee's. James C. asked Lottie if she had gone on any trips with the church lately, and Lottie said, "No, but we are going to Kentucky next month to see the Ark."
　　James said, "Oh, they found it?"
　　At the time I had a mouth full of coffee, and I came close to spewing it on everybody. —*Juli C.*

Bad Shot

Earl had squirrels in his attic, so he got his shotgun, went up, and shot a hole in his roof! —*Ralph J.*

Bad Gas

Will was putting three-year-old London down for a nap and he passed gas. London said, "I mell dat. I don't like dat mell!" —*Suzanne R.*

Them Busbees

On Thanksgiving Day, London would not take a nap, so she was cranky. We were getting ready to go to our big family dinner, and she did not want to go.

I told her, "You'll get to see all your family."

She asked, "What's their name?"

I told her, "Busbee."

London said, "I don't like dem Busbees."

—*Suzanne R.*

Suzanne, Will, Aden, & Silas

Trick-o-Treaters

Back in the early seventies, Twiddle and I talked Ralph and Walter into dressing up as women and going down to Uncle Bub's house to trick or treat. Bub answered the door, took one look at them, and said, "Damn, Mary, they get bigger every year!" —*Lottie G.*

Cold Water

Wyatt and Gage came by the house, and they were wearing shorts. The weather was still very cool, and I asked if it was not too cold for shorts, and they said no.

Wyatt said that he had already been in the water!

I said, "Are you crazy?"

He said, "I didn't plan to get wet; I was kayaking, and a snake fell in the kayak, and I jumped in the water!"

I asked, "What kind of snake was it?"

He said, "I didn't take time to find out!"

—*Aunt Jewell*

Grandpa's Goat

When Grandpa lived at Pearson's Pond, he had a goat. This goat followed him around like a dog. When Grandpa got in his boat to fish, the goat got in with him. He also came into the house and watched television with Grandpa, and if he saw something that excited him, he would butt the TV. —*Lottie G.*

$20 Ring

It was Valentine's Day, and Johnny came into my home office, pulled out his wallet, took out a $20 bill, and laid it on the desk. He said, "I did not know if I should get you flowers or candy, so just buy what you want."

I grabbed the money and told him to come with me. I took him down to the jewelry store, called Myra over, pointed, and said, "I'll take that ring, and this is the down payment for it." I handed her the $20 and said, "Johnny will be in every week to make a payment until it's paid for!"

She insisted I wear the ring home. Johnny never did make a payment; I had to pay for it myself! So, when I show off my ring, I tell people that Johnny paid $20 for it! —*Maria B.*

Packed Plymouth

When I was a boy in Edgefield, a small circus came to town. A local car dealership had brought out a big old Plymouth and to show how roomy the back was, they took out the back seat and had about twenty boys get in. Then they put a donkey in! That donkey and we boys were stepping all over each other trying to get out!
—*Ralph J.*

"Do not give me advice. Help me!" —*Old Saying*

Hearing Loss

I was at the doctor, and he was examining my knee, which I had just had surgery on. He had his head down and was mumbling. I thought he was praying for me, and I thanked him. Later, my daughter-in-law Michelle told me that the doctor was not praying for me, he was dictating into a recorder that was in his pocket!
—*Pealey H.*

"Well, suck-it-up, buttercup!" —*Marty L.*

Whole House Alarm

I was at my son Chris's house —Michelle had gone to work. By habit she turned the alarm on as she went out. I was alone with the kids, who were asleep. I walked into the living room and the alarm went off. A loud voice could be heard above the shrieking saying, "INTRUDER IN THE LIVING ROOM! INTRUDER IN THE LIVING ROOM! IDENTIFY YOURSELF! IDENTIFY YOURSELF!"

Well, I panicked and said, "I'm the mother in-law!" I thought quickly that I would call Michelle and have her turn

Chris H.

the alarm off. Then I remembered that my cell phone was on the table outside on the deck! I ran out, got it, and came back in.

NOW the voice is saying, "INTRUDER COMING IN THE BACK DOOR! INTRUDER COMING IN THE BACK DOOR! IDENTIFY YOURSELF.

IDENTIFY YOURSELF!" Then the voice said, "WE'RE CALLING THE POLICE!"

I screamed, "NO! NO! DON'T CALL THE POLICE!"

About that time my fifteen-year-old Grandson came in and turned the alarm off. Boy, was I upset! Chris later said he had watched it all on video on his cell phone, and I sure looked funny! I did not think it was funny at all! —*Pealey H.*

Call Ned

We were having breakfast at Hardee's and Walter got up to leave, saying "Y'all be good, and if you have any trouble call Ned!" —*Juli C.*

$40-a-Month Rent

After I turned eighteen, I was working for my stepdad making $12 per hour. My mom told me that I would have to start paying $40 a month rent! WELL- I got mad, quit my job, packed my bag, and left. The only money I had was $36 in change. I got a job at a fast-food restaurant making $6 an hour and moved in with my friend and his family. They lived in a 600-square-foot house with no heat or air. I had to sleep in the hallway on the floor on an old mattress. It was so cold in the wintertime that I would let their big dog sleep with me just to stay warm. The only food I had was what the restaurant was throwing away at night. **And I had to pay $200 a month rent!** After a year, I joined the Navy, had a bed to sleep in, three meals a day, and they paid *me*! —*Jordan P.*

Jordan & a good meal

Aunt Lottie

The day before Aunt Lottie's funeral, I was delivering some flowers to the funeral home. I parked, got the flowers, and went to the back door. There was a casket sitting there. I got upset, thinking that my Aunt Lottie was in the casket! I got my cell phone out and called Eddie the owner and asked, "Is that my Aunt Lottie outside baking in the hot sun!"

Eddie said, "No Vicki, she's inside." —*Vicki B.*

Vicki B.

The Fruit Cake

Back in the eighties at our Thanksgiving dinner, we decided to have an auction. Well, every year Lottie would bake a fruit cake for Johnny. This year someone came up with the idea to auction off the cake, knowing that Johnny would not let anyone have it. When the bidding started, someone bid $5, then $10. By then everyone is hooting and hollerin'. Now Johnny knows what is going on. The bid keeps going higher and everyone is cheering Johnny on! $25 - $30 - $40 - $50 - $60 - $70 - $80! Johnny won! He then swore that he would not share one bite with anyone! —*Juli C.*

The Prize

I got the prize for being the best speller in the third grade, three years in a row! —*Robert B.*

Medicare Insurance

I kept getting these calls from an insurance company asking to speak to Gail. I told them they had the wrong number, but that did not work. They kept calling! Finally, one day they called, and I said, "I am sorry to tell you this, but Gail has died, and she has gone to be with the Lord. The whole family is in mourning."

The salesman said, "I'm so sorry, we won't call again!" —*Josh N.*

Huffy Bicycle

I got this call from a telemarketer trying to sell me an extended warranty on my vehicle. I told him, "The other night I was drunk as Cooter Brown, hit a tree, and totaled my car. And that was my third DUI. So, unless you can insure my Huffy, we do not have anything to talk about!" —*Josh N.*

Josh at about four years old

Retirement

After working for the same company for forty years and them trying to get me to leave the last ten years, I finally decided to retire. On my last day as I was leaving the plant, I mooned the security camera! —*Tommy M.*

"The best time to plan for your retirement is before your boss does!" —*Anonymous*

Going To Church

One time I decided to start going to church with Mama and Lottie. I went for two Sundays in a row to the church that our cousin Earl preached at. After the second Sunday, I went home and was cooking dinner when the doorbell rang. It was Cousin Earl. I opened the door and said, "If you have come to visit as Cousin Earl then you are welcome. In fact, you can stay and eat with us. But if you are here as Preacher Earl wanting to save my soul, then you are not welcome!" —*Marty L.*

Good Tipper

I was in a restaurant today, and the waitress told me and my friends this story. There was a group of people at her table, and she asked to whom to give the check. Well, they started arguing about who would pay. This little boy spoke up and said, "Give the check to my mom. She is the best tipper!" —*Juli C.*

Cemetery Address

After my husband Joe died, I kept getting phone calls from people wanting to talk to him. I would tell them that he was not here, but that did not satisfy them. Finally, I told them where he was staying. I gave them the address of the cemetery! They never called back. —*Carmen C.*

Hauling Moonshine

One night back in the thirties, I was hauling a load of shine. I was going down this long hill on Vaucluse Road (it was dirt back then). I was going wide open, about twenty-five miles an hour, when a carload of blacks pulled their car out in front of me, and I hit them! They all jumped out and ran. I grabbed a jug of liquor from my car and ran! Back then you did not have license tags, so there was no way for the sheriff to know who the vehicle belonged to, and it was cheaper to get another car than to go to jail and have to pay a fine! —*Rob B.*

Killing Weeds

After church today, I was talking to my friend Lee. I asked what she was doing this afternoon and she said, "I am killing weeds. I bought me a propane blowtorch and I am going to burn them!"

I started laughing and said, "Dang, girl, you are serious about this."

She said, "My husband John said, 'Are you not overthinking this!"

I told her, "Don't let John use that blow torch. You know how men are; he may burn down the house!"
—*Juli C.*

Rubber Snake

Deana had been having trouble with chipmunks digging in her flowerpots, so she bought some black rubber snakes to scare them away. She would move the snakes around from place to place. I was walking across the patio and saw that all the stuff from her square wooden table was now on the chair, and the table was tilted over. So, I set the table back and put the stuff back on it. Being OCD, I like things in proper order. The next day, I came across the patio again, and all the stuff was moved back to the chair, and the table was tilted over again! I started moving it back when I saw a rubber snake. I picked up the snake, and it wrapped its body around my arm! I nearly came out of my skin! That snake was alive! What I did not know was that Deana had called the exterminator to come spray for spiders, and she wanted him to spray under that table.
—*Kelley W.*

New Rims and Tires

We were living in Louisiana. Ken was sixteen years old and had worked hard to buy himself a car, a Nissan 280 Z. He was so proud of that car! He then saved up $1,000 and bought new rims and tires. One day I saw a bunch of concrete blocks on the side of the driveway. I assumed that Joe had put them there. Joe saw the blocks and thought that I had put them there. The next Sunday morning, Ken got up early to go to work at the country club. He had to be there at 5:30 AM. He went out to get in his car, and he had no wheels! Someone had come during the night and jacked the car up and taken his wheels, and the car was sitting on the concrete blocks! We do not know who put the blocks there, but we now know why. —*Juli C.*

"Never ask a tire salesman if you need new tires!" —*Anonymous*

The Pleasure of Going to Walmart

My local Walmart used to have twelve cashiers. Now they only have two, except when they are really busy. Then they only have one! —*Juli C.*

Being a Politician

My choice early in life was either to be a piano player in a whorehouse or a politician. And to tell the truth, there's hardly any difference. —*Harry S. Truman*

"We hang petty thieves and appoint the great ones to public office." —*Aesop*

I Will Show You

When Tom was little, he wanted to spend the night. I told him no because his grandpa and I would be the only ones there, but he insisted on staying. I told him if he stayed, he would not be able to go home. He said okay and stayed with us. When it got dark, Tom wanted to go home and wanted me to call his mama to come get him. I told him that I did not know her number. He said that if I did not call, he would take his britches off! I said that was okay, I had seen little boys' behinds before. —*Nora B.*

When I came home from a date that night, there was Tom, asleep with his little hinny sticking up! —*Marty L.*

Code of Conduct

#1 Tell the truth. (Squeal only if you were the wrongdoer.)

#2 Blame someone else. (If you were the wrongdoer.)

#3 Deny any knowledge of wrongdoing.

#4 Say nothing. (This was used most often.)

Great care must be used in #1 and #2, as there is always a backlash from your siblings.

Mama never did break the code, but she solved the problem by lining us up and whipping all of us. "This way, I know I got the right one!" she would say.
—*Juli C.*

"It is always best to tell the truth, unless you are an exceptionally good liar." —*Anonymous*

Playing Poker in The Barn

When I was twelve years old, Aunt Tinkey came and got me to babysit her three mean children. She wanted Uncle Ed to take her shopping. She drove back to her house and when we got there, Uncle Ed was in the barn with some of his friends and playing poker. Well, she got mad, went, and got the shotgun, and shot the side of the barn. Men scattered every which way! Uncle Ed came out and took her shopping. —*Juli C.*

"If you think no one cares about you, try missing a few car payments!" —*Once Heard*

Trip to Gatlinburg

Back in 1986, I met Mama, Daddy, Lottie, Johnny, Maria, and their kids at a cabin in Bryson City, North Carolina. Now, I had been to the mountains many times but never to Gatlinburg, so Daddy said he would take us. Well, we all piled up in the two cars, with Daddy driving the lead, and we headed for Gatlinburg. What a beautiful ride. There is no place like the Smokies. We drove for a couple of hours, and Daddy pulled into an overlook. We all got out and walked to the edge of the mountain. Daddy pointed down and said, "Well, there she is." I was excited. I could not wait to get there and do some shopping! We all got back in the cars and took off. After a while, I started thinking that it was taking a long time to get there. Next thing I know, we pull up to the cabin in Bryson City!

I said to Daddy, "I thought we were going to Gatlinburg!"

He said, "I told you that I would show it to you."

Pa was a man of few words. —*Juli C.*

Fire In Her Pants

The family had been to Clark Hill for a day of swimming and picnicking. On the way home, I felt something biting me on my backside. I had a bee in my bathing suit! I screamed and jumped all over the front seat trying to kill that bee. When I got home it felt like I had fire in my pants! —*Lottie G.*

The Fish Were Biting

Bony Grandma was fishing. She had on this big ole straw hat. Bobby would throw rocks. Everywhere he threw a rock, Grandma would throw her line, thinking it was a fish. —*Johnny B.*

"I have enough money to last me the rest of my life unless I buy something." —*Jackie Mason*

Counting Cows

When Ken and Jerry were small, Sue and I would play this game with them in the car to keep them from fighting! We put the boys in the back seat, Ken on one side and Jerry on the other. Whenever they saw cows on their side of the road, they would count the number of cows. Whenever we passed a church with a cemetery on your side of the road, you had to bury your cows and start all over again. At the end of the trip, the one with the most cows won the game. Whenever Jerry had to bury his cows, he would get upset and just sob! We had to quit playing that game. —*Juli C.*

Little Horse Creek

We kids loved to see Aunt Tinkey come to visit in the summertime. She would load us kids in her car and take us to Little Horse Creek to swim. That creek had the coldest water on earth! The Duncan kids, who lived just up from the creek, would come down. We would all have a great time. The Duncans had a little girl who looked just like Winkey. One day we were getting in the car to leave, and Lottie picked up this little girl (thinking she was Winkey) and put her in the car. The girl started screaming! Lottie had the wrong kid! —*Juli C.*

Peaches

Bobby and I went to Trenton with Grandpa Leopard to buy peaches. On the way home, Bobby and I sat in the back of the truck and threw peaches at signs and mailboxes. Grandpa pulled off to the side of the road and said, "Who threw that dad burn peach!?!"
—*Johnny B.*

"Start off each day with a smile and get it over with." —*W. C. Fields*

Grandpa's Business

When Jewell and I were teenagers, we both worked in a drug store in Aiken. We would take a taxi to Grandma and Grandpa's house and wait for Daddy to pick us up after he got off work. Well, Grandpa had decided to open a curb market in the front yard. They lived on a busy highway. Grandpa built his market and put a drink machine in it and filled it with dopes (Cokes). He was not quite ready to open for business, so he kept it locked. Well, I knew how to pick locks. So, each afternoon I would pick the lock. Jewell and I would get us a Coke, then go up to Ms. Riley's store and buy peanuts to put in our Cokes. After a month or so Grandpa checked out his supplies, and his Coke machine was empty! He sure did get mad! —*Lottie G.*

The Dream

In the seventies, Mama and Daddy did not believe in banks, so they kept what little money they had at home. One night Mama had a dream that the house had burned and all their money was gone. She asked Lottie to take her to the bank and open an account. Two days later the bank burned! Mama was terribly upset until Lottie explained that the money was insured. —*Juli C.*

Done Good

We went to the egg farm and Daddy bought fifteen dozen eggs for Easter. When we got home, Mama said, "You done good. You only broke five dozen!" —*Carl B.*

"Insanity is hereditary. You get it from your children." —*Anonymous*

Huhanne Hicks

One fall when Suzanne was three years old, a group of us went to the mountains to see the autumn leaves. It rained all weekend, and we spent a lot of time inside the cabin. For entertainment Suzanne would sing for us. She had a little Fisher Price camera and would say, "Airy body smile!"

Robert would ask, "What's your name?" and she would tell him "Huhanne Hicks" So to this day Robert still calls her that. —*Katie W.*

Huhanne Hicks

"We live in an age when the pizza gets to your house faster than the police!" —*Once Heard*

Learning to Drive

The summer Marty and I stayed with Micky and Pealey was very eventful. Mickey tried to teach Marty and me how to drive his VW and truck (both stick shifts). With much hard work and long hours, Marty was able to conquer the lawn mower! I, on the other hand, was not able to master anything. I still cannot drive a straight shift! —*Katie W.*

Must Have Been a Mistake

Joseph came home from school with a bad conduct report. I asked him if he was misbehaving, and he said, "No.

I said, "Your teacher said you were." Then in an effort to not call his teacher a liar, Joe said, "It must have been a mistake, Wahburt!" (He called me by my first name.)

I said, "There was a mistake, and you just made it!" He got a spanking. —*Robert B.*

Smoking In the Pine Thicket

Robert, Carl, and I got some cigarettes and went behind the house in Edward C.'s field where there were some thick young pines. We smoked for a while, then went home, leaving our cigarettes and matches in the thicket. Well Robert got to worrying about it, so he went back to the thicket, and next thing you know, he set the pines on fire! We would have been in big trouble if it had not been for the fact that the field belonged to Ed C.
—*Ned B.*

Poison Oak Alert

I was out in the woods scouting for a deer hunting place. When you are in the woods, trees and bushes are used as an outhouse. When I returned home, I had small bumps on my legs, arms, and belly. The next day I realized I had poison oak! It was on my neck, arms, legs, back, stomach and even on my Yakidoo! My bride told me that when they were kids and got poison oak, their mother would put a few capfuls of bleach in their bath water to dry it up. So, I thought if I dabbed bleach on it, it would heal faster. IT DIDN'T!

Ronnie B.

When I got up the next morning, my Yakidoo was swollen four times the normal size and was as red as fire! For days, it was swollen. I finally went to the doctor and got antibiotics. You know, when the swelling went down, that thing peeled like a snake! —*Ronnie B. (Huck)*

Crossing The Tracks

Every time Grandpa took me home in his old black truck, we crossed the railroad tracks, and he would say, "The train just came by."

I would ask, "How do you know?"

And he would say, "Because he left his tracks."

—*Leigh B.*

Leigh B.

Store-Bought Potato Salad

When I was in college, I would go up to Bryson City, North Carolina, with Grandma and Grandpa and stay at the Royal's property. Each day, we would take a picnic and go to Deep Creek. One day we stopped at Ingles grocery store and bought potato salad to go with our sandwiches. That was the worst potato salad ever! Those potatoes were cut into big chunks and were not thoroughly cooked. We carried the potato salad back to the cabin. Grandma gave it to the caretaker's dog. That dog ran up and down that mountain all night, howling! We figured it gave that dog gas! To this day we will not eat store bought potato salad —*Joni M.*

Jordan's Knife

Kelley, Deana, and Jordan were out shopping, and Kelley bought Jordan his first pocketknife. While they were in the car, Jordan was in the back seat, and Kelley gave Jordan a lecture on knife safety. At their next stop, they got out of the car. Deana took Jordan's hand and it felt wet. She looked down and saw that Jordan's hand was covered in blood! He had cut his hand several times while Kelley was giving him a lecture on knife safety!
—*Grandma Juli*

Grandpa Busbee and Me

Grandpa Busbee was a man of few words. He always looked serious, but he did like to pull pranks on some of us. One day while in the woods, he found this melted compact (the mirror was still good). Johnny was visiting South Carolina, and when he came back home to Florida, he brought me a present from Grandpa. You guessed it. It was that mirror. The next year I wrapped it and sent it back to Grandpa, then he sent it back to me. For years, we exchanged this gift! —*Carmen C.*

Tater Pie

It was twelve degrees at 4:00 AM when I left the house with my friend Rodney. We were meeting Pa at his house at 5:00 AM. As we walked in the back door, we could smell the aroma of breakfast. Pa was cooking and said, "You boys sit down and eat." He poured me a cup of coffee that looked like black shoe polish. I know that it had boiled for twenty minutes on that old stove. We ate fast. We were excited because we were going hunting at the Buzzards Roost.

As we got ready to leave, I noticed Pa packing a sack. He put it in his hunting vest, then grabbed his gun and said, "Times a-wastin' boys. Let's go."

Out on the porch Pa said, "Ain't no need for all of us to drive. Y'all just ride with me."

We grabbed our guns and equipment and threw it in the back of his old pickup. Seems like forever getting to the Buzzards Roost. When we got there, we put our hunting stuff on and headed for the woods.

Pa put me on a big old rock overlooking a creek and said, "I'll see you at lunch time, son." I could just see my hand in front of my face when I heard Pa say to Rodney, "Climb up in that stand and be still."

I knew that I had better not move if I ever wanted to come back with Pa again. The time that I spent on that rock until lunch turned out to be the longest six hours of my life! I was so cold, everything in my body shook, including my teeth. I thought I would freeze to death!

About 9:30 AM, I saw a shaft of sunlight and prayed, "Lord, let it shine on me." I was so cold I could not feel my feet, hands, ears, or nose. Now it was 12:00 PM, and I heard Pa coming up the bottom. The only things I saw alive that morning were two ole squirrels.

Pa came by and said, "Let's go, boys." I tried to get up, but my legs would not work. It took five minutes before I could walk. Finally, we got to the truck that was parked on this old country road. Rodney and I lay on the ground in the sunshine trying to get warm. I could not wait for Pa to start the truck and turn the heater on.

To my surprise, Pa opened the door, reached behind the seat, and pulled out the same sack I had seen him put in his vest earlier. He sat on the ground by us, then Rodney said, "Mr. Busbee, you about ready to go home?" to which Pa responded, "Boys, y'all didn't bring any lunch?" and we said, "We thought we were going home for lunch."

Pa said, "Boy's, y'all better get a piece of this tater pie, it's a long time till dark."

Rodney and I ate that tater pie like it was the last morsel of food on earth. We looked at each other without saying a word, wondering what our wives would think because we promised to be home right after lunch. I never rode with Pa again as long as he lived. Although, we hunted many times after that.
– *Micky H.*

Battle Of the Gully

Many years ago, in a place called Jordantown, there lived three families—The Busbees, Cosnatans, and the Coopers. Up the road a way lived the Carters, cousins to the Busbees. These families came together to make the wildest bunch you ever saw. Miss Lottie and Miss Jewell were the roughest two gals you ever came up against. Why, when they got together with their brothers Walter B. and Johnny B., and their Cousin Earl, they would fight like Indians, mean Indians, like the kind that would take people and cut their hair off, pull their skin back. Real mean, you see.

Earl C.

One time the Cosnatans and the Coopers met together to stage an ambush.

There was a big gully that ran from the Busbees all the way down to the Cosnatans place.

They waited for the wild bunch to come down the gully. What they did not count on was the wild bunch figured something was up. So, they went around behind and attacked. It was a bloody battle, and when it was all over, everyone went home so they could fight again another day. —*Earl C.*

The Camp-Out

Chris and Cousin Tom shared a unique friendship from toddler age. They did not get to spend much time together except in the summers. They were in the sixth grade this particular summer. Tom was coming to the country to spend the weekend, and they planned to camp out. They wanted to build a fire and cook hot dogs with no interference from us. Since it had rained for a few days prior to the camping, we felt it was safe to let them build a fire, so we gave them the matches. They made many trips to the kitchen before settling in for whatever they were doing. The next morning, they both appeared, anxious to watch Saturday cartoons. They did not get far before Mickey stopped them. They were so black, only the whites of their eyes could be seen. Their story was, they could not find any dry wood to burn, not even the pine straw. So, they resorted to a rubber tire! By their faces we wondered if it was them that had been roasted instead of the hot dogs! When Mickey insisted they take a bath before sitting on anything, their reply was, "But we didn't do anything to get dirty!" —*Pealey H.*

Black Powder Deer Hunt

My Daddy and I went deer hunting, he with a muzzle loader, me with bow and arrow. We were hunting at White Oak Ridge, and it was loaded with acorns, a deer's delight. Sometime around eleven or twelve o'clock, I heard Daddy shoot. I waited for half an hour, then went to see what he had. When I got there, he was still sitting on his ladder stand, and his face was black.

I asked, "Where is he?"

Daddy said, "I didn't hit him."

I said, "How do you know if you didn't look?"

He said, "When the smoke cleared, he was still standing there eating acorns."

I asked, "Did you try to reload?"

"Yes," Daddy said, "But that was too much. Ole trophy decided that I might get lucky the next time, so he hit the trail." —*Rob and Walter B.*

Watching TV and Cussing

Leah was five years old, and we were watching a movie on TV.

At one point Leah said, "What the hell was that?"

I asked, "What did you say?" and she repeated, "What the hell was that?"

In a stern voice I asked, "What did you say?" and Leah said, "What was that?" —*Ken C.*

Kicking Clothes

When we were kids, we would take the shoe lash (iron tool used to repair shoes, which was heavy) and put it in the middle of the floor, put some dirty clothes on it, and watch as people went by and kicked the clothing out of the way. —*Lottie G.*

The Black Cat

There was this big black cat that took up at my house. He would eat my cat's food and beat him up. I got tired of this, so I put that cat in a crate and took him to Langley Cemetery. As I let him out between Ed and Tinkey's, Gene and Helen's graves, I told him, "Go fight with them. They all like to fight." The last I saw of that cat; he was cutting it down between the graves. —*Lottie G.*

Persimmon Wars

When we were kids, we spent as much time in the woods as we could because when we were at home, Mama would make us work. We would take limbs and trim them up, then put a sharp point on one end, then put a green persimmon on the sharp points, and throw the persimmons at each other! It sure did hurt when you got hit. Chinaberry trees were great. We made necklaces from the green berries and hula skirts from the leaves. We would make blow gun ammo from the berries. We would also cut long limbs, trim them up, tie strings on the fat ends, and those were our horses. We rode those horses all over those woods! —*Juli C.*

Vidalias

When Tom was nine or ten years old, he came to visit us for the weekend. I fixed him and Chris a sandwich for lunch and put onions on them. Tom asked if they were Vidalias. I said, "No."

Then Tom said, "We only eat Vidalias at our house." —*Pealey H.*

Fourteen Children

Someone at church asked why my parents had so many children. I said, "You know, I asked my mom that same thing one time. After she backhanded me across the face, she said, 'That's none of your business.' So, I do not know the answer." —*Juli C.*

Big Nose

Jim was at Mead Hall School teaching little kids how to play soccer, and this little boy came up to him and said, "I can see up your nose!" —*Carole W.*

Frances the Mule

When I was about thirteen years old, Walter and James C. talked me into riding Frances. They put me on her back and then whacked Frances across the rump with a board. Off we went, down across Mr. Byrd's field with me hanging on and screaming for dear life. Frances went down through the gully that was full of briers, then up the hill into the pine thicket. I do not remember anything after that! But what I do know is that I am a quick learner; I never rode that mule again! —*Juli C.*

The Spanker

My granddaughter Kaity was born stubborn. About once a month her dad would have to spank her. One day after she had a spanking, her five-year-old brother said, "Kaity, why do you do that? You know that he is the biggest, the meanest, and the spanker!"
—*Grandma Pealey*

"A Zebra never changes his spots." —*Al Gore*

Boobies

We were at a museum in Florida —Ken, Leah, Pealey, and me. Leah was about five years old. There were lots of old master's paintings of women who were nude on top. Leah asked her dad why all those women were showing their "boobies." Later as we were going from one building to another, there was a bridge that connected the two. It had fancy railings and statues along the edge. Ken saw the nude statue of David up ahead and very quickly picked Leah up and got her to look the other way while he hightailed it as fast as he could past David. —*Grandma Juli*

Ken & Leah

"I love deadlines. I like the whooshing sound they make as they go by." —*Doug A.*

Long Denim Skirt

I was going to a party in Birmingham, and it was cool weather, so I had on boots and a long, straight, denim skirt that had a slit in the back. As I was going up the walk to this house, there were two old women behind me. I heard one of them say, "Just look. That skirt is cut all the way up to her yahoo!" —*Juli C.*

Ducks, Ducks, and More Ducks

One Easter someone came up with the idea of buying ducks for all the little kids. Deana refused to let Jordan take his home! He cried all the way back to Knoxville. There sure were a lot of "Mad Mamas" that day.
—*Grandma Juli*

Jordan & Grandma

Summertime Fun

One summer I had Katie (three years older than Deana) come stay with Deana and Ken while I worked part-time. I came home one afternoon, and Katie was hosing Deana down! They were bored with watching TV, so they and some neighbor kids found a pretty big puddle in the dirt road and decided to play in it. First, they splashed through it. Then Ken and a neighbor boy rode their bikes through it, peddling really fast then hitting the brakes just as they got to the puddle, sliding and splashing mud! Then they just got down and rolled in it! I did not have the heart to fuss at them. —*Mom Juli*

Deana & Katie

"As far as anyone knows... we are a nice normal family." —*Anonymous*

"And now, this edition ends. If there is to be another, that depends on my wacky family coming up with more stories." —*Juliana H. Chase*

Acknowledgements

I want to thank all my family for the fun times we have had together over the years. I look forward to Thanksgiving and Easter when we have our family reunions each year. We tell stories and laugh non-stop; I go home exhausted from laughing. Thank you to my brothers Walter, Johnny, Robert, Ned, Huck, and our late brothers Carl and Bobby. And to my sisters Twiddle, Pealey, Winkey, Katie, and Marty, and our late sisters Lottie and Doll. I love you all.

A special thank you goes to my children, Deana and Ken, my grandson Jordan and granddaughter Leah, and my son-in-law Kelley (my TV fixer). I am so blessed to have y'all in my life.

Thank you to all my cousins, nieces, nephews, and friends for sharing your humor. This book would not have happened without you. And a loving thanks to my artist friends Bonnie and Donna, who are always there for me. Love you both.

And lastly to my mom Nora and dad Rob. Without them, there would not be an "Us."

About the Author

Juli Chase grew up outside a small town in South Carolina, one of fourteen children. The woods were their playground. They were very inventive when it came to having fun. The community they lived in, Jordantown, had about fifteen houses, so everyone  knew everyone. She married and moved to New York, then lived in eight other states. During that time, she established a successful art career.

Juli's work is in the permanent collection of The Smithsonian Institute, National Museum of Women in the Arts, Tennessee's Governor's Mansion, and corporate and private collections throughout the U. S. and six foreign countries. She is the author of *Front Porch Memories*, a family cookbook with stories. She continues to paint and write at her home in Knoxville, Tennessee.

www.ingramcontent.com/pod-product-compliance
Lightning Source LLC
Chambersburg PA
CBHW070241010526
44107CB00041B/1481/J